ABO COVER

For over 2,000 Sundays Robert Holton's voice could be heard all over the state of Alabama, the country of Belize and throughout the U.S. via GBN saying: " 'For the word of God is quick, and powerful, and sharper than any two-edged sword, piercing even to the dividing asunder of soul and spirit, and of the joints and marrow, and is a discerner of the thoughts and intents of the heart.

Neither is there any creature that is not manifest in his sight: but all things are naked and opened unto the eyes of him with whom we have to do.' The Living Word brought to you by the Woodlawn Church of Christ in Birmingham, Alabama and now your speaker Jerry Jenkins." This verse was very important and special to Dad. The picture on the cover is his Bible opened to that verse.

THE
LIVING
WORD

*Sermons of
Jerry A. Jenkins*

*Compiled by
Jeff & Dale Jenkins*

ISBN-13: 978-1523679041
ISBN-10: 1523679042

Published by The Jenkins Institute

thejenkinsinstitute.com

Cover design & interior layout: Joey Sparks
Professional editing: Kathy Jarrell

To Preachers Everywhere

"For after that in the wisdom of God the world by wisdom knew not God, it pleased God by the foolishness of preaching to save them that believe" (1 Corinthians 1:21).

Dad loved his fellow preachers. He thrilled at their successes and hurt when they hurt. So whether you preach full-time or part-time, whether you've been preaching many years or are just starting out; whether you preach in a large church building in a modern metropolis or a thatch hut in a third world country; whether you struggle every day with your preaching or you are at total peace in your ministry; with love, we dedicate this book to you.

May God's richest blessing be yours is our prayer for you.

ACKNOWLEDGEMENTS

There are many key people who have helped in getting this book to press and we want to recognize their assistance here.

It starts really with Jean Owens. For 35-40 she was dad's secretary. She transcribed most of the notes you will find in here and filed them away for some later use. She kept dad turned in a right direction and wrangled his crazy calendar. She took tens of thousands of calls and messages and was a top-notch assistant.

Joey Sparks continues to amaze us. His keen eye toward design, his eagerness to help and his willingness to put up with our "we need it now's" have earned him a place on the TJI Wall of Fame. Now, if we just had a building with walls to hang the picture, he'd be gold.

Sue and Brittany Erwin stepped up to the plate and did the work on about six of these sermons that we only had in tape form. They volunteered joyfully, and were encouragers in the process.

We also acknowledge Freed-Hardeman University, Harding University, Faulkner University, Polishing the Pulpit, and Pepperdine University for allowing us the use of manuscripts of lessons delivered at each of these places.

CONTENTS

JERRY AUSTIN JENKINS
January 15, 1936 - October 26, 2010

"God Speaks Today" & "The Living Word" are both phrases that became synonymous with the name Jerry Jenkins. He passed from this life on October 26, 2010, at the age of 74 surrounded by his family. "Jerry was as focused on Jesus more than any man I've ever known," were the words used to describe him by one friend of many years.

Jerry was born on January 15, 1936, in Huntsville, Alabama to John & Geneva (Bates) Jenkins. He had one brother (Dan) and two sisters (Barbara & Dot). Jerry graduated from Athens Bible School.

He attended Freed Hardeman University (AA), David Lipscomb University (BA), Harding Graduate School of Religion (MA), Alabama Christian School of Religion (MT), and Abilene Christian University (DM). For a time, Jerry served as Dean and Greek Instructor for Alabama Christian College of Biblical Studies.

Jerry and his High School sweetheart, Mamie Frame were happily married for nearly fifty years. Mamie encouraged him in every good work in which he was involved. They had four children, Jeff, Carey, Dale, and Melissa. They also had nine grandchildren and five great grandchildren. During the last two years of his life Jerry was married to Mona Eason.

During the early years of his preaching life Jerry worked with churches in Truman, Arkansas and Hamilton, Alabama. For the last forty-four years of his life he preached for the Roebuck Parkway Church in Birmingham, Alabama.

Jerry spent his life being involved in numerous good works. He was a builder. The works he helped establish show that he loved people of all ages and all backgrounds. He was the founder of Maywood Christian Camp in Hamilton, Alabama. He directed a week of camp each year and served on the Board of MCC until his passing.

Jerry was cofounder of Jefferson Christian Academy in Birmingham. He believed strongly in Christian education. He served on the board of JCA until his death. Along with these boards Jerry also served on the Board of Directors for Rainbow Omega and the Advisory Board for Freed Hardeman University. He was also the President of the Tuthill Foundation.

Jerry had a passion for mission work. He and his wife Mamie were the first missionary couple to Belize, Central America in 1969. He directed sixty-four campaigns and spoke for all of them throughout the country of Belize. In addition he conducted radio and TV programs throughout the country of Belize. He baptized and developed a long time friendship with brother Melvin Davis who serves as the preacher for the Belize City Church of Christ. Jerry conducted over 100 evangelistic campaigns and preached for each of them during his life.

Shortly after moving to Birmingham to work with the Roebuck Parkway Church (at the time it was known as the Woodlawn Church), Jerry began a weekly television program. He hosted

The Living Word television broadcast for forty-three years. It became the longest running religious broadcast in the state of Alabama. The Living Word was shown throughout the state of Alabama and around the world on the Gospel Broadcast Network.

Jerry's greatest passion was soul-winning. He conducted thousands of Bible studies using the Jewel Miller Filmstrips. Early in his preaching life he developed a special "close" to be used following each film. These "closes" are still being used today. He once said that he baptized every person he studied with who invited him into their home for a meal. For many years the Roebuck Parkway Church averaged baptizing one person every week.

Not long after he began making mission trips to Belize, Jerry developed a Bible study that he felt would be best suited for the people of Belize. "God Speaks Today," became the primary tool for teaching the people of Belize for many years. Many souls were won to the Lord through the teaching of God Speaks Today. This study continues to be used in mission trips to Belize.

Besides God Speaks Today, Jerry wrote the following books. God's Plan for Life, Lovingly Leading Men to the Savior, Fundamentals of the Faith, Principles From Paul, The Church that Jesus Built, Do You Love Jesus, and Go into All the World. He also contributed chapters for many other books and articles for numerous publications.

Jerry Jenkins loved the Lord and the Lord's Church. He loved people of all ages, social standings, nations, and all walks of life.

He exemplified what it means to be a Gospel Preacher and a man of God. His life could be characterized as a life of humility, grace, concern, and love.

He is greatly missed by his family, the Roebuck Parkway Church, the people of Belize, and everyone who knew him. As his friend said, "Jerry was as focused on Jesus as any man I've ever known."

PREFACE

No book we've published has been as agonized over as this one because:

> The volume: We have thousands of dad's sermons.

> The emotion: Every time we read a lesson, we see Dad in his easy chair   studying, dozing, reading.

> The "pride;" this is Dad's stuff. We want it done well.

A few notes about Dad's preaching:

1. He believed simply and pure-heartedly in the Scriptures. He did not tamper with or dismiss. If the Bible said it that was it.

2. He began with some comments

3. He liked a good joke or story but did not build his sermons around them; but around the Word.

4. He often used material he gleaned from other sources.

5. He was gentle in language but bold with Truth. He spoke what he believed needed to be said, but always with kindness.

6. Most of his sermons were on a few simple things--salvation, going to heaven, the truth of Scripture, Evangelism, Church growth.

7. Evangelistic: Dad's preached pleading for and expecting responses. He was always looking for someone to teach.

For the most part we will leave the sermons as they came to us. We want you, the reader, to get the full effect of the sermon. Some are transcripts and some are from Dad's notes.

Before a number of the sermons, you will see a few notes explaining a little more about the sermon and why it is included. We hope these sermons and the corresponding stories will add to the interest of the material and let you see some into the heart of Dad.

Be kind!! What is
(kindness)??

I need this lesson!! that
I find in my life
if I am stressed, worried
about something, tired, hungry,
... you get the picture ....
one of the first thing to
go is kindness

BE KIND

takes its place –
— irritation w/ others
getting under my skin

— become snappy
— frown instead of smile

— lash out

basically – if things aren't going
my way, I tend to take
it out on others,

Every preacher has his favorite sermon. Whether it's that first sermon you felt you "owned" or your "try out" sermon, it's your go-to. We're not sure we can prove it, but for Dad one nominee would have to be his kindness sermon. He preached it for over 40 years. It was his "go to" sermon for Bible classes to kick off a Gospel Meeting. We think it was his favorite because:

1. We heard him preach it so much: Ask any of the kids and they can finish "Two gun Kelly..." or "Cold knuckles..." or "I wish you was my Daddy..."

2. But just as much important is that Dad embodied this sermon. Whether the man made the sermon or the sermon made the man—the best one word to describe Dad would be "kind." He was kind to all. In all our years we can barely come up with a handful of times we saw him angry.

J & D

It is an honor to be invited to be with you in this series of gospel meetings. I hope that you will endeavor to make every possible opportunity to attend all of the sessions that you possibly can. I know you will. We thank you so much for the privilege in preaching here once again. I am always a little bit leery when someone asks me to speak to the second gospel meeting. Maybe like this one preacher I heard about this church had this practice annually of firing their preacher and hiring a new one. This went on year in and year out where every year they would fire the preacher and hire a new one. Finally they hired a young fellow to come and preach for them which was me and at the end of the first year I had my resignation all written out ready to hand to the elders but they surprised me by saying we would like for you to work another year with us. Well, I did and at the end of two years I was assured they would fire me but low and behold they said we would like for you to work another year. This went on several years and finally I could stand it no longer and I said please tell me why it is that annually you had the practice of firing your preacher and hiring a new one until I arrived. Low and behold every year you have asked me to stay and work another year. One of the elders spoke up and said well we didn't want to tell you but since you have asked, several years ago the elders here found out this church just does not like good preaching and said you are about the nearest nothing we can find. So I have been more than 40 years at the same church there and it is quite a joy and honor to be there.

This is a Bible study hour and I always appreciate a little more being less formal and I would like for us to sing another song. A great song this morning. Perhaps you heard it, I have heard it a number of years ago. A song by brother Andy T. Richie, Sr., "Lord lay some soul upon my heart and love that soul through me." Let me kindly go over it with you and you join in when you can.

[Jerry sings]

"Lord lay some soul upon my heart and love that soul through me. And may I nobly do my part to win that soul for thee."

Wouldn't it be great if we could all just practice that? "Lord lay some soul upon my heart, love that soul through me and may I nobly do my part to win that soul for thee." How long has it been since we have lead a soul to Christ? Well, a gospel meeting gives us an opportunity to invite somebody to attend service. I was a young preacher, probably 18 or 19 years of age and I was invited to conduct a meeting in Noble, Arkansas. I went up and stayed with a lady, Ms. Chastain. At that time she seemed real old. She was probably in her late 60's. It doesn't seem very old now, but at that time I thought she was ancient. I arrived on Saturday evening and she said, "Well I am going to ask my neighbor one more time. I know it will not do any good. I have asked her for the last 15 years to attend the services and I know it won't do any good to ask her, but I am going to invite her one more time." Low and behold, the dear lady came. She came back the following night and the next night. Before that meeting was over, I believe it was on a Friday night, we had the opportunity of baptizing her into Christ. I am glad Ms. Chastain did not get discouraged and stop. If you have been inviting your neighbors and friends for 16 years, let me encourage you to invite them one more time. Try to encourage them to come and to be a part.

He was the most notorious gangster that New York City had ever produced. He would just as well shoot a man as to look at him. On one occasion, Two Gun Kelly was surrounded by the police. He exchanged gun fire and in that gunfire he was mortally wounded. They found a note that was inside of his shirt pocket. That note says, "Within me there beats a weary heart, but a kind one." Are you a kind person? Does your wife believe you are kind? Does your husband believe you are a kind person? I believe a lady that lived on a block, 2-3 blocks over from where I lived, was a lady that was perhaps the most unkind person that I had ever known. She came to services Sunday morning, Sunday night and she came Wednesday night. She taught a little class for children. She attended the Ladies' Bible Class on Tuesday morning. I had an idea that if you asked the people on that block to vote as to who was the meanest person on the block, she would have won very easily. It is possible for us to take the Lord's Supper on a regular basis, which I believe we should, to sing praises to God, to give of our money, and yet for us to be unlike the Lord wants us to be in the lifestyle we live. This morning what I am challenging us to do is to be kind. My wife says that I am always kinder after preaching this sermon, so it may not help any of you, but it will help me to be a kinder person.

Are you a kind person? The word kindness is an interesting word. It occurs some 48 times in the King James translation of the Bible. The Bible says that love is kind. One of the ways you can identify whether you are a loving individual is whether you are a kind individual. This morning, in the brief time we have together, I want to mention 5 reasons that you need to be kind.

There will be a test that will be given at the end of class to see how many of those you can name. You are allowed to take notes.

Five Reasons Why You Need To Be Kind:

1. I need to be a kind person because God is kind and I want to be like God. The Bible often speaks of the kindness of God. I know there is an aspect of God, the wrath of God and the anger of God, but I am also aware that the Bible often speaks of the kindness of God. It is said in Genesis 39:21 God was kind and dealt kindly with Joseph when He allowed him to become the Prime Minister of the country of Egypt. It was said in the writings of David, Psalms 31:21 Blessed be the Lord, for He has shown His marvelous kindness. Psalms 117, which contains only 2 verses, is the shortest chapter in all of the Bible. David said, "Praise the Lord all you gentiles, laud Him all people. For his merciful kindness is great toward us. The strength of the Lord endureth forever." Praise the Lord! In Luke 6, the Bible says, "Love your enemies." This is Jesus speaking. "Do good and lend, hoping for nothing in return. Your reward be great and you will be sons of the Most High, for He is kind to the unthankful and to the evil." Even when we are not living as we should, God is still gracious and kind to us. Even when we walk contrary to His divine will, the Bible says that God is a God of great kindness to us. I would have known of the kindness of God, even I think if the Bible had not said that God is kind. I would have known of the kindness of God when I awake in the morning and I see the beauties of the sunrise; or perhaps, even last evening as we were driving toward this place. We saw one of the most beautiful sunsets I believe I have ever seen in all of my life; or maybe you know when you stood on the beach and you watched the waves

as they pounded the surf; or perhaps, when you were in the Smokies in the fall of the year and it appeared that God had taken His majestic brush and painted a scene that defies description; or maybe in a little town called Delphi, in the country of Greece, sticking above the mountain peaks, there in its heights and you look down to the clouds that are below you. We would have known of the kindness of God perhaps, even if the Bible had not informed us that the God that we serve is a God of great kindness. Whenever I am unkind, I am unlike God. I am not a Godly individual when I lose my temper. I am not a Godly individual when I become angry and I say things that I should not say. When I mistreat family members and when I mistreat my neighbors or friends, I am not a very Godly person. The Bible informs us that God is a God of great kindness.

One cold, wintry night a little boy and a little girl, poorly clad, made their way up to a big old farm house. Cold knuckles wrapped on that door and after a while a rather large lady, but with a smile on her face, came to the door. She saw two little children outside. They were cold. She brought them in before the big fire burning in the fireplace. She hurried off and got a big glass of hot chocolate. She came and put a blanket around their shivering shoulders. The little girl looked up into her face and said, "Are you God's wife?" Our God is a God of great kindness. May God help all of us to be kinder individuals. Jesus said in Matthew 5:16 "Let your light so shine before men that they may see your good works and glorify your Father, which is in Heaven." So we can be kinder people. Reason one, you got it? You need to be kind because God is kind.

2. I need to be kind because I am commanded to be kind. The Bible commands me to be kind. The Bible does not say be kind when you feel good. The Bible does not say be kind if you are able to pay all of your bills on time. The Bible does not say to be kind if you are making the kind of grades you desire to make. But, the Bible does say we are to be kind. In Colossians 3:12 "Paul said, "Therefore, as the elect of God, (you are the elect of God. I am speaking to the elect of God in this assembly this morning.) holy and beloved, put on tender mercies, kindness, humility, meekness and longsuffering." Put on (clothe yourself). We spend a lot of time preparing, don't we? We want to look as good as we possibly can. If that tie doesn't match, we want to exchange ties. You ladies, you have to spend a little time, I've noticed, looking into the mirror every morning. You are not any more vain than men are. We try our best to look the very best we can. Paul said, "as you dress yourself,"as you attire yourself, in your spiritual life there are some things I desire for you to put on. Among those things, I want you to put on this attribute of kindness. In Ephesians 4:32 the Bible says, "Be kind, tender-hearted, forgiving one another even as God for Christ's sake has forgiven you." He just flat out tells us, we are to be kind. He did not make it optional. He just said, I want you to be kind. I command you to be kind. Be tender-hearted. Be forgiving in nature, even as God, for Christ's sake has forgiven you. I am to be a kind individual because God commands me to be kind. Real and genuine Christianity produces kindness. It does not make one rough. The principles of our Savior will not make one crabby or sour. It does not make one disposed to violate the proper rules of politeness and courtesy. I know we are living in a society today and in a culture today, where to be gracious and to be courteous to one another is perhaps almost a forgotten art.

you could look at these last ones as selfish reasons. But we shouldn't see kindness as something that we give away and can't keep for ourselves. You don't empty yourself

There is no religion in a sour temper. There is none in rudeness. by There is none in stiffness and repulsiveness; none in violating being the rules of good training and good upbringing. I need to be kind. kind because I am commanded to be kind. You have any doubts? I am commanded to be kind. Sometimes it is hard to be kind instead isn't it? I pulled up at the anytime teller. I was in a big hurry. you. The person put their card in about three or four times. Maybe benefit they couldn't remember their pin number. Finally they got it to as well, operate properly. They got the money out and they sat there and counted all of their money. It looked like they were writing some notes or something. Finally, I had just had it. I beeped my horn about three or four times. They looked back and it was one of the members there where I preach. I was rather embarrassed to say the least. We need to be kind because we are commanded to be kind. You need to be kind because you represent Jesus. You are God's servant and therefore need to be kind.

3. In the third place, I submit to you that you need to be kind because kindness will get the desired result. That is what the Bible teaches. That kindness will work. There was a fellow that was really no account. He was about as sorry as you could ever imagine anybody to be. He would curse and swear at the drop of a hat. Many people had gone to see him and visit with him, but it was to no avail. Finally, the man became ill. He still wanted nothing to do with those "church people," as he called them. His little boy came in to see him. His son said, "Dad, I know what they are saying about you. They say that you are mean and ugly. They say you are sorry and not fit to live, but Dad, I want you to know that I love you with all of my heart." None of the other things worked. However, the message from this young boy was a message that turned this man's life around.

Caused confusion. Connie them to be love cruel and rise to your level

"Kill them w/ kindness" Cause discomfort by treating someone w/ extreme kindness

I had an aunt and an uncle that lived in Owens CrossRoads, Alabama. I don't know whether you know where that is or not. It his up near New Hope, Alabama and around Gurley, Alabama (out in that area.) I used to go and be with my aunt and my uncle. I thought that hoeing cotton was a lot of fun. I would go out and hoe cotton for 10 minutes and have a really big time at it. I thought it was a lot of fun to pick cotton. I would go out there and pick for an hour and then they would give me money for picking that cotton, until Mr. and Mrs. Flemming moved up close to where we moved. One fall, Mrs. Flemming said to my mother and Dad, "We are going to take our children out to pick cotton this fall. Would you like me to take your children?" We did. We went out every day. We had to wait until the dew dried before they would weigh the sack. It was all I could do to pick 100 pounds. I don't know whether I even reached that stage or not. It was difficult indeed. There was a girl there that could pick nearly 200 pounds. That aggravated me because that girl could pick more cotton than I could pick. I am saying to you today that kindness is a quality and a characteristic of life that we need to live because it will work. I went out and visited my aunt and uncle. My aunt Low was a member of the Lord's church. She was faithful. She would walk two miles to the little church called, Glovers Chapel. She WALKED two miles. She would go even when it was raining. She would go when the temperature was below freezing. She would walk. My uncle George would hitch up the mules and the wagon to take her to town on Friday to Owens Cross Roads store about three miles away. But, he never offered to take her to services. The preacher would come by to see my uncle George and he would be very rude. "What's wrong preacher? Contributions getting a little low? What did you come after?

Why are you here?" But low and behold, she went out. The day came when he became a new testament Christian. I would like to tell you it was because of a great sermon that I preached, but that was not the reason. He lived with a godly woman for all of these years. He became a very, very faithful member of the Lord's church. A rich Bible student. In 1st Peter 3:1-4 Peter said, "Wives, in the same way be submissive to your husbands. So that any of them do not believe the Word, they may be won over without words, but by the behavior of their wives." When they see the purity and reverence of your life, your beauty should not come from outward adorning or braided hair, the wearing of gold jewelry or fine clothes. Instead, it should be that of your inner self. The unfading beauties of a gentle and quiet spirit, which is of great worth in God's sight. I want to suggest to you that we need to be kind because kindness will get the desired result. I have often heard that you can lead and old horse to the water, but you cannot make him drink. I said that somewhere, I don't remember where it was. After the services were over, there was a dear lady that came to me and she said, you can make him drink. I said, "Sister, I don't think so. I have heard that all my life. You can lead an old horse to the water, but you cannot make him drink." She said, "If you give him enough salt, he will drink." Jesus said you are the salt of the earth. He was talking to me. He was talking to you. He said you are the salt of the earth, but the salt can't its savor by being mean-spirited and unkind, by being faultless and people of ingratitude.

"It is henceforth good for nothing, but to be cast out and trodden under the foot of men. You are the light of the world, a city set on a hill whose light cannot be hidden. Neither can men light a kindling, put it under a bushel, but on a candlestick that

A gentle answer —
Proverbs 15:1

it may give light to all who are in the house." Kindness will work. I have a friend who is a preacher. If I call his name, you would know him. So I will not call out his name, as that would be unkind. I remember this friend went to a store and a restaurant. He did not get the kindest service (after all he is mister important.) He did not get the kind of service that he thought he should receive. So, he gave the waitress a piece of his mind. He told her off pretty good (not profanity,) just ugly and mean-spirited. He called the manager over and then gave the manager a piece of his mind as well. The manager said to brother so-and-so, "I know you are busy and all. I would like to apologize for you having to wait so long and I would like to just give you this steak free of charge." He said, "You know what I did? I got up and walked out." I said to him, "Did you invite him to come and hear you preach next Sunday?" I know that was not very kind of me, but I think sometimes we need to have a reality check. We went down to Shoney's there in Roebuck where they used to have a Shoney's. It was after the 6 p.m. Sunday night service and a group of us were eating chocolate cake with chocolate syrup poured all over it and whipped cream on the top. Man, it was good. The lady looked somewhat distraught. I said, "I guess you have probably had a hard day today." She said, "You would not believe it." I said, "Well maybe you had a hard day, but these people they have been good to you, no doubt?" She replied, "You would not believe Sunday is the worst day of our service here. Those folks come down from singing about how they love Jesus and pray and sing as well as all the other stuff they do up there. Then they come down here and you would not believe how they treat us." I said, "Yeah, but maybe they tip you good?" She said, "We get less tips on Sunday than any other day of the week." Well, we need to be kind because we are to be an example. The Bible commands us to be kind. Are you a kind person? I need to be kind because God is kind. I need to be kind because The Bible commands me to be kind. I need to be kind because kindness will have the desired result. It will help you to lead a soul to Christ, to restore a soul that is lost in sin. I need to be kind. *how do you really feel when you know you've been rude to someone? compare that to*

4. I need to be kind because of the good feeling it gives me. *how you feel when you've gone out of the way to be kind* Kindness just gives you a great feeling, a wonderful feeling. Who is the most miserable person this morning, (joking, do not raise your hand.) I do not know who you are, but I do know something about you. The most miserable person here this morning who is someone that is selfish. Selfish people are miserable people. I visited Mrs. Miller. She was 85 years of age. She was in a nursing home. She did not want to be there. She had a nice home. She had been able to drive herself around. She had done well in life. But, now she was in a nursing home, perhaps abandoned by her family, to some degree. Her children did come about every other week to visit with her. Yet, she was a very gracious and pleasant person to be around. I said to her on one occasion, "Why is it that you can be so pleasant, when most of the folks I see in here are just grumpy and grouchy?" She said, "Whatever you were before you got in this place, you will be after you arrive her." I have often thought there is a lot of truth in that isn't there? We need to understand that when we serve others and look to others, it will so enrich and mold and shape our lives. It will make us happy individuals. There was a man who drove his Lincoln Continental home from work. He saw a little boy standing outside of a grocery store crying. He pulled over to the curb, touched the button and the power window came rolling down. He said, "What's wrong son?" He

kindness isn't just for the other person. It is for you too. You benefit from your own kindness

said, "Nothing mister." He said, but I knew little boys did not cry unless something was wrong. The big man got out of his car and said, "Son, tell me what's wrong." He said, "Mister, my Dad sent me down here to by some things and on the way down here, I lost my money. I have looked everywhere to find that money, but I cannot find it. I have been back and forth several times, but it is not there." The man said, "Well go tell your Dad what happened. Everything will be alright." The boy said, "Mister, you do not know my Daddy, he will beat me." The big man took the little lad by the hand and went into the grocery store. He bought the necessary items. On the way out, he stopped and bought a big ole candy bar. He gave it to the little boy. The little fellow went running out the front door of the store, but just in a few minutes, he came running back. He threw his little arms around the big man and said, "Mister, I wish you was my Daddy." The big man said I must have driven 25 blocks looking for a little boy who had lost his money. If you are unhappy, why not serve others. Why not assist others. Why not begin to think of other people, rather than think that the world needs to revolve around yourself. I need to be kind. I need to be kind because God is kind. I need to be kind because I am commanded to be kind. I need to be kind because kindness will work. I need to be kind because kindness will give me a wonderful inner feeling of peace. No wonder Jesus was happy because he was so kind to others. Oh I know He could be a tyrant. In Matthew 23, he calls Him a bunch of snakes. I understand that. But, look at his life. For those that needed a friend, He was indeed a friend to them. He was so kind.

5. There is one other reason we need to be kind. We need to be kind because kindness will always come back to us. Galatians

When you are kind, people remember it and will be kind in return.

6:7 "Be not deceived, God is not mocked. For whatever a man sows, that he will also reap. He that soweth to his flesh, shall of the flesh reap corruption. But, he that soweth to the Spirit will of the Spirit reap life everlasting." It will come back. We will reap what we sow. But you know that we will reap more than we sow. Every gospel preacher has a stack of cards that encourage him to keep on keeping on. Someone was thoughtful and someone said "you made a difference," in my life. We think that one sermon can make that difference. They were sitting on the left side as I stood and faced the auditorium. They had been half-hearted members of the Lord's church. They were both highly successful. She was in charge of a hospital unit there in Birmingham. He was a highly successful engineer.

That Sunday morning, they came down the aisle and they made some changes in their lives. As far as I know, they have never missed another Sunday morning, Sunday night or Wednesday night service, unless they were sick. They tell me that the one lesson made a difference in their lives. So, we believe sometimes you know that one lesson can make a difference in a person's life. You are going to reap what you sow. If you sow ugly, mean attitudes through the world, that is exactly what you are going to reap. But, if you will sow kindness, it will come back in many, many different ways. Well, you might say, "What can I do?" Some of us might getting up on the right side of the bed for a change. One lady was asked if she had woken up grouchy this morning and she said, "No, I just let him sleep." Some of us are not fit to be around until we have had our coffee, or whatever. So, we need to be gracious and kind to others. It will come back to us in so many marvelous ways. Maybe there is someone who needs a visit from you. Maybe there is someone who needs a phone call. Maybe there is someone who needs a word of encouragement from you. It does not take a great deal of effort. It is not expensive, but what a difference it can make in our lives. So, we are to be kind because we will reap what we sow.

"Dear Mom and Dad,

Many times I have sat down to write this letter. I did not have the words and I do not have the words now, but I want to thank you for all you have done for me. Dad, I remember when brother and I were dating that you allowed us to have the automobile on Friday nights. You walked 20 blocks to work and back. We will never forget that. I remember when you took me to the football game. Just as our team was about to score a touchdown, which would have made a difference in the game, I pulled on your pants leg and said, "Dad, I gotta go to the bathroom." You didn't scream and holler and shout. Other Daddies do not act like that. I have been with Bill's, Jim's and Frank's. When you came to visit us at college you had on that old blue suede suit. I said, "Dad, are you going to wear that old suit?" You said, "We older guys do not have to impress the young ladies like you young fellows do." But, I know now it was because you had two boys in college and you could not afford any better. Mom, what I remember about you...I remember you were always happy. We took clean socks and underclothes, always in the right place for granted. I remember that big ole black wash pot and scrub board. I remember that you were always singing."

The old couple said, "We own our own home. We have a couple of vehicles. We have some investment, but we would not take everything we own for this letter from our son. Be kind and tender-hearted, forgiving one another, even as God for Christ's sake has forgiven you.

Let us close in prayer:

Gracious Father, thank you so much for the privilege that You give to us of being students of Your word. We thank you Father for the great truths regarding kindness. We pray that You would give us the attitude of heart and give us the Spirit within us that we will be kind and caring individuals. Help us Father to be better mothers and fathers, grandparents. Help us to be kinder to our brothers and sisters. Help us to be known for our kindness to others. We are grateful Father that you are a God of great kindness. We thank You for the instructions that You have given to us in Your word.

In the name of Jesus we pray.

Amen.

USE OF TELEVISION IN PREACHING THE GOSPEL

In the summer of 1966 Dad held a meeting in Birmingham, Alabama at the Homewood church. During the meeting the Homewood elders met with Dad and offered him the pulpit which was open there. The Woodlawn church not too far away was also looking for a preacher and invited Dad to meet with them. At that time Homewood was larger, growing faster and offered him more money BUT Dad really only had one question for both churches. Would you consider a weekly TV program to preach the gospel. Homewood did not think they could but Woodlawn said they would. Dad took the job at Woodlawn. And in 1966 Dad left a healthy work he loved in the secure little town of Hamilton and moved his 9 months pregnant wife and three young sons to the most racially divided city in America because he believed he could reach more people with the gospel there than anywhere else.

In 1967 Dad began "The Living Word" with his theme song "How Great Thou Art" and narrator Robert Holton of Abilene, TX doing the intro. For over 40 years Dad preached on television. His program became the most watched locally produced show in the state as well as the longest running. In over 40 years he never repeated a show. Anywhere he went in Alabama he was recognized and respected. We do not know how many letters he wrote, questions he answered, Bibles he gave away, transcripts he mailed or souls he reached via television but that work more than any other kept him at Woodlawn/Roebuck Parkway.

Thanks to several, but most notably Jean Owens we have the transcripts of many of those sermons. They reveal the simplicity with which Dad preached - sermons on faith, belief, the church, Christ, grace, kindness, heaven, hell. The sermon that follows is a treasure found. It is the transcript of a lesson Dad presented in 1971, four years into "The Living Word" on The Use of Television In Preaching the Gospel.   *J & D*

It is Sunday at 12:30 and you are just coming in from a wonderful period of worship to God. As you enter your home, you hear the telephone ringing. You pick up the phone and a nurse on the other end asks for you. She informs you that a patient on the fifth floor at University Hospital is holding a nurse at knife point and says he will only speak to you He knows of you only through television.

It is 10:30 Sunday evening and your telephone rings. A man on the other end states he feels a real need to discuss God's word with someone. Following a study, you have the privilege of baptizing him into Christ about 12 A.M.

These are two dramatic moments which have been the result of our television broadcast, now it its fourth year.

Recently Dr. Don Durgin, President of NBC Television Network, in an address before the Hollywood Radio and Television Society in Beverly Hills, California, stated that last year the average American Family watched television five hours and fifty minutes daily. For the seventh consecutive year, an increase occurred. Americans invested 3.8 million dollars in new television sets.[1]

Value of the Television Program

Jesus commissioned us to preach the whole gospel to the whole world. We should use every method available in fulfilling our Lord's commission. Television offers the unique advantage of combining audio of radio, the continuous performance of theatre and the electronic techniques of film.[2] It is capable of fusing the best of all previous communications media.

A second value is that you will be permitted to enter the homes that otherwise it is impossible to enter. You can enter the homes of the educated and the uneducated, the very wealthy and the very poor. There is a value even in the secrecy which shrouds a man sitting in the privacy of his own home. Here, with no pressure, he can think about his relationship to God.

Some might object to paying thousands of dollars each year to preach on television. A careful study will reveal that using television, one can reach the largest possible audience in the shortest possible time in the most economical and effective way.

A fourth value is that television offers opportunities of open doors for those participating in such programs. Numerous speaking opportunities in the community are granted and honors of recognition are given by a high caliber program. The image of the church is enhanced and untold good is done from a public relation standpoint.

One real value of mass communication is to find those seeking the truth and help them toward a more perfect understanding of God's will. Practically any soil can be cultivated to receive seed, but it requires time. It is urgent that we locate those most receptive to God's word and that they help us reach others.

Another value of such programs is that it contributes to the personal work program of a congregation Not only will it help those who immediately contact you about studying the Bible, it also offers the advantage of future study. Many times the door has almost been closed when a personal worker would say, "By the way, have you seen our television program?" and they would become more receptive to cottage meetings and Bible correspondence work.

Quality of the Television Program

The quality of the program cannot be over estimated. There is time available on many television stations if our approach to the station management and the quality of our program is high. More and more VHF channels are being approved by the FCC. As of June 30, 1968, one hundred sixty-seven additional VHF channels have been granted construction permits.[3] Most television stations are deeply concerned about the ratings of their programs. It is no secret that when a religious program comes on, many sets go off or changed to another program. This can be offset if the programs are made attractive enough and if a congregation is willing to spend sufficient amounts in advertising the program. Show the station management newspaper ads and mailouts which are planned to promote the program. They like to have their station mentioned often to the people of the community they serve.

It is my suggestion that the intro and closing of the television program should be done professionally. It may cost a congregation hundreds of dollars, but in the long run, it will pay higher dividends. The set itself; that is the furniture used on the program, will be provided by the station. It would be much better for the congregation to spend several hundred dollars to have an attractive set where the program is produced.

The Follow Up

We should not be content merely with the fact that the gospel is being preached to thousands. Though, with the proper type of television program, one can have the effect of sitting down in the living room with his friends, there still must be that personal contact. For this reason, note the following suggestions:

1. Some offer of a tract or Bible Correspondence Course should be given on each television program.

2. Telephone numbers should be given to indicate where someone could call immediately at the close of the program for help.

[1] Don Durgin. "The Worst of Times on the Best of Times," Vital Speeches of the Day, XXXVII, No. 6, Jan. 1, 1971, pp. 186, 187.

[2] Robert L. Hilliard, Writing for Television and Radio (New York: Hastings House Publishers, 1962), pp. 13, 14.

[3] Charles S. Aaronson, 1970 International Television Almanac (New York: Quigley Publications, 1969), pp. 534.

I'M JUST A
NOBODY

Dad's life centered around a very few things but ultimately even the things his life centered around (local church, Belize missions, television, schools and education) all led back to ONE thing. Dad wanted everybody to go to heaven. He was not just a preacher or a minister the best description of Dad is that he was an evangelist.

He hated to be out of town because it took him away from one on one Bible studies with lost people. In 1995 Jeff's wife Laura had a life-threatening surgery and Dale and Dad made the trip from Alabama to be with them. The stay lasted several days. After a couple of days Dad would leave for a while by himself. One afternoon Jeff, Dale and Dad left the hospital to grab some sweet tea. When we went into the Hardee's the waitress knew Dad already. Where he had been going was to find someone he could develop a connection with and the waitress knew Dad because he had set up a Bible study with her. He couldn't stand going that many days without studying with someone. If he ever got "sharp" with preachers it was preachers who spent their lives in the office and never conducted Bible studies with lost people.

Everything he did seemed to be focused on this one thing. This sermon, presented at Polishing the Pulpit in 2004, and the one that follows epitomizes his heart.

J & D

It is indeed an honor for me to be with you this afternoon; I thank you very much for the invitation. You've grown quite a bit since I was on the program last and first couple of times I was with you and what a tremendous number that are present and we are very grateful to see the growth and the interest in this session. I'm happy to have with me today Brother Kyle Massengale who has just joined us at Roebuck Parkway he's, many of you may know him, he is a lawyer and Assistant District Attorney formerly before he was employed with us, so if any of you have any legal problems he's the man to see and I'm sure he can raise his hand, Kyle they want to see who you are, right over there, alright and we're just really honored to have Kyle working with us at Roebuck Parkway.

I thought about maybe just getting up and reading the title than sitting down, I mean that's some more title. "I'm Just a Nobody Trying to Tell Everybody About Somebody that Can Save Anybody". I don't know whether that's original, but my, my what a topic. I want to begin today by reminding you of the Apostle Paul's statement in Romans chapter 1, Paul said "For I am not ashamed of the gospel of Christ: for it is the power of God unto salvation to everyone that believeth; to the Jew first, and also to the Greek." Because of the power of this gospel Paul would say I am dead both to the Greek and the Barbarian both to the wise and to the unwise and as much as in me is I'm ready to preach the gospel of those of you who are at Rome. As much as in me is, Paul was a proclaimer of the word publicly but Paul also went from house to house teaching the Word of God.

I hope this afternoon that I might be able to say something that it would encourage you my fellow preaching brethren and those of you that work at various capacities as soul winners for Christ that might inspire and stimulate us to realize the great joy and the privilege that we have of being children of God. I want to begin today by reminding us all that God is an amateur. The word amateur is a Latin word, it is a word which means just for the love of it and I'm convinced that we all need to be amateurs and we need to be effective servants of God simply because we love the work. Alex Rodriguez third baseman for the New York Yankees makes over 25 million/annually. The minimum salary of an NFL player is $225,000 his first year, it doesn't take him long before he is right at that million dollar mark. In the NBA Kevin Garnett with the Minnesota his salary is in excess of 25 million dollars/annually. When I was growing up in Huntsville, Alabama a group of us would get out, near where I lived in an open field, field with sawdust and we would play football without helmets, without shoulder pads, without any of the equipment. You know why we did that because we amateurs. We did it just for the love of it, just because we wanted to. I've often thought if I were God I can make some changes and I speak respectfully; but if I were God I could do away with golf on Sunday. I'd let a man hit the ball 300 yards through the week but on Sunday he'd only dribble it about ten yards [congregation laugh]. If I were God and I speak respectfully, I would do away with fishing on Sunday. I'd let a man catch as many fish as you can imagine through the week but on Sunday he wouldn't even get a nibble. But that's not the way it operates, pick up your paper and you'll notice that Mr Bass and his son went fishing and caught the largest string of the year, last Sunday morning about 11 o'clock. If I was God I could do away with working on Sunday. I'd let it rain right up to my friend's farm and then I'd cut it off and after a while he'll get the idea but that's the way God is. The Bible teaches that God is an amateur. He does things just for the love of it.

For example the Bible says in Ephesians 2:8 "For by grace are ye saved through faith; and that not of yourselves: it is the gift of God." In Titus 2:11 "For the grace of God that brings salvation has appeared to all men." In Hebrew 2:9 "But we see Jesus, who was made a little lower than the angels for the suffering of death, crowned with glory and honor; that he by the grace of God should taste death for every man." In 1 John 4:8 "He that loveth not, knoweth not God; for God is love." Never was there a more important declaration made than this, never more crowded in just a phrase than this particular concept—that God is love. In the darkness of the world of sin in which we live, sorrow is so prevalent among the races and we are assured that God is love and there are many passages in the word of God that speak of this love and I would of course be perhaps somewhat negligent not to remind you. Deuteronomy 7:8 "But because the Lord loved you, and because he would keep the oath which he had sworn unto your fathers, hath the Lord brought you out with a mighty hand." Psalms 146:8 David said, "The Lord openeth the eyes of the blind: the Lord raiseth them that are bowed down: the Lord loveth the righteous." And to the inspired writings of Moses and David, Jeremiah penned these words (Jeremiah 31:3) "The Lord hath appeared of old unto me, saying, Yea, I have loved thee with an everlasting love: therefore with lovingkindness have I drawn thee." John 3:16, "For God so loved the world that he gave his only begotten Son, that whosoever believeth in him should not perish, but have everlasting life." In Romans 5:8, "But God commendeth his love toward us, in that, while we were yet sinners, Christ died for us." Ephesians 2:4, "But God, who is rich in mercy, for his great love wherewith he loved us" 1 John 3:1, "Behold, what manner of love the Father hath bestowed upon us, that we should be called the sons of God."

But God is an amateur, God does things because of His love. Now you know there's a sense in which we are professionals, isn't there? because most of us here today receive a salary and so as I reflect about whether we are professionals there has to be some difference and that difference is that we not be a hireling, that we not be content to simply draw a salary and be involved in a job as there are a lot of folks involved today without any real depth of love for the lost and I have known my preaching brethren and I love every one of them but I've known those that I believe came very close to being a hireling. Oh they would preach on Sunday morning about the necessity of going out and teaching one's fellow man but one friend of mine said I've been at this church for 16 years I've never taught anybody unless they came to the office or unless they call me on the phone and ask that I might teach them the gospel. Brethren it's been our joy at Roebuck Parkway to baptize, according to most, one per week for the last 38 years and it has not come simply because we've held services on Sunday morning and had a sign up saying, "Here we are, you lucky sinners, you found us." Our great desire is to go out and to teach others the unsearchable riches of Christ and in humility today I ask you my brethren why don't you make a promise, a vow to God that you will spend at least one night for the rest of your life out knocking on doors and be an amateur for God; just simply be out there and be concerned.

The Bible says in 2 Corinthians 4 "For we preach not ourselves, but Christ Jesus the Lord; and ourselves your servants for Jesus' sake. For God, who commanded the light to shine out of darkness, hath shined in our hearts, to give the light of the knowledge of the glory of God in the face of Jesus Christ. But we have this treasure in earthen vessels..." Why in the world did God put the treasure in earthen vessels? Why did he not put it on the lips of angel who could perhaps speak so much more eloquently than can any of us? He tells us, "... that the excellency of the power may be of God, and not of us." That's why we have the gospel in earthen vessels, old clay pots and that's what we are, old clay pots and we need to be amateurs we need to be doing the work in which we are involved just simply because we love the work not be a hireling or a professional that draws a salary by simply presenting a lesson on Sunday morning that he may be have gotten off the internet somewhere or Sunday night but being willing to get out and to knock on those doors, to be sure that every unsaved person within the congregation where we work has the opportunity to receive a visit and instruction.

Roger Thompson in commenting on the verse in 2 Corinthians told about when he was a young man that he worked at Brinks Armored Car Company in San Bernardino and they often ship tons of coins from Las Vegas. His job was to wrap these coins up and one day he and the office manager were alone in the building and they got a call from the Bank of America, they were in a panic, they had 4 hours to get the change over to the bank but all of the armored trucks were out on that particular day. The manager backed his own '49 Ford pickup into the loading bay and he and Roger stacked $25,000 worth of coins into the back of that old '49 pickup truck. Please picture two men driving down in an old 1949 pickup truck loaded with money and when they arrived the manager pulled up to the curb, he jumped out and said we'll have to get a dolly to carry this money, you wait here in the truck and he waited there in a neighborhood where folks would slit your throat for a few dollars but nobody bothered him, no one ever noticed because the treasure was so packed in such a commonly way. God says we have this treasure in earthen vessels that the excellency of the power maybe of God and not of us. The great soul winners are not always the fellas that are the most educated. I know within our congregation I think of a man that lead 13 people to Christ one year not too long ago. If you tried to pick out up an ideal soul winner, in all probability, he would not be in your top 10 category. I know a guy that stutters when he talks, who has lead numerous people to Christ and so I know it's not skill, it's not ability. I'm convinced that the thing that really makes the difference is what's in our heart is that desire.

We are a nobody you're a nobody, you're a nobody, you're a nobody and it is your job because you are nobody not because of the degree titles that you have behind your name and I'm not knocking education, not simply because of a you know how you may be able to dress, the automobile you may drive but simply because you're an old clay pot with a treasure that's worth more than the billions and billions of dollars of our world, trying to tell everybody, trying to tell everybody the gospel is for everybody. I had a little trouble in dividing these points up about everybody and anybody but let me just simply try to make this distinction for everybody would be that the gospel is for every person. In Matthew 28:18 "And Jesus came and spake unto them, saying, All power is given unto me in heaven and in earth. Go ye therefore, and teach all nations, baptizing them in the name of the Father, and of the Son, and of the Holy Ghost: Teaching them to observe all things whatsoever I have commanded you: and, lo, I am with you always, even unto the end of the world." In Mark 16:15, "And he said unto them, Go ye into all the world, and preach the gospel to every creature." You know there's no one that's unimportant in the eyes of God and everybody in our world deserves to hear the gospel of Jesus Christ and it is our task to go into all the world and preach the gospel to everybody, to that person that waits on you at the store, to that man that helps to pick up your garbage twice a week or once a week, he has a soul and he deserves the same message that you've been privileged to hear. The gospel is to be for everybody one of the problems that I have is I forget this. I get in my own world, with my own problems and I forget about the nobody's in the world, I forget about the fact that the gospel is for everybody and all of us have had the experience, haven't we of being successful and seeing somebody obedient to the gospel. I know a man that was injured in the Korean War, he came back, he has missing one arm and one leg and he has a house because of the funds that he received as a result of his injury. He has a house it's unbelievable, he has a room almost as large as this room with a big ball down there and he used to bring his girls in and so forth and he told me he said you know I spend about $250/week and he heard the gospel, he accidentally just said I wonder if I go visit that church and he came by one day and somebody went out to see him, set up a study with me and as a result of that the man obeyed the gospel and he had a question for me, he said you think it be alright for me to give $250/week, that's what I've been wasting. I was afraid our brethren would get to him and tell him you don't have to give that much to be a faithful Christian [congregation laugh]. He's a nobody, a nobody that's really made a difference in the world in which we live, responsible for so many people being lead to Christ. Everybody has a right to hear the gospel and then I need to tell everybody about a somebody and think about the greatness of Jesus. In Hebrews 2:9, "But we see Jesus, who was made a little lower than the angels for the suffering of death, crowned with glory and honor; that he by the grace of God should taste death for every man." Romans 8:9, "But ye are not in the flesh, but in the Spirit, if so be that the Spirit of God dwell in you. Now if any man have not the Spirit of Christ, he is none of his." And so think about what Christ has done for us. More than 1900 years ago on a Thursday evening prostrate up on the ground crying out to God oh my father if it be possible let this cup pass. Nevertheless not my will but thy will be done. I was in a graduate class and I guess it'll be alright to identify, Harding Graduate School and in that particular class somebody pointed out that God just arbitrarily chose the methodology of redeeming men.

I do not believe that I believe the only price that could have been paid was paid and there was no other way, Jesus paid the price and he paid that price for you and for me and then they took our Lord and they tied Him to that whipping pole and they scourged Him, they beat him worse than you would beat an animal, they made a crown of thorns probably would thick sharp thorns and hard as nails and they implanted it in his head. Then, Pilate realizing the innocence of Jesus tried to get off the hook and he brought out the most hardened criminal that he could find a man that probably started out sassing his mom and Dad and maybe at first saying words that he shouldn't say and then later perhaps cursing and swearing and eventually stealing little objects and then eventually according to the Gospel of Mark, he was one who lead an insurrection, he was a murderer, he was an old hardened criminal and Barabbas said where were the two of you that I released and they cried out that they wanted Barabbas released. The word Barabas "bar" meaning son and "abbas" a name often applied to God, perhaps a Jewish mother when this little boy was born might have thought this boy will be the Messiah, how disappointed she must have been but this man took the place of Jesus and when Pilate said, "And what should I do with Christ?" They said, "Let it be crucified."

A cross beam weighing more than 150 pounds and a man had to take that cross and they drove those nails as they extended Christ upon that cross through his hands. Hands that lifted little children in his arms and blessed them, hands that touch the Leopards, hands that were placed upon Peter's mother-in-law and recovered her from illness, hands that lifted the sinking Peter whose faith failed on the tempestuous Sea of Galilee, hands that caused the blind eyes to open and the voices that had not been able to communicate in a lifetime to speak and hands to take our sins and cast them into the depths of the sea and they raised that cross and they jarred it into that ground and we need to walk the Via Dolorosa in order that the chill may be taken out of our hearts and that we might be warm with the zeal for service. I read about a certain nominal church member sitting at ease in Zion, she had a dream and she dream that she knocked on the gates of the Celestial City the question was asked who is it she identified herself and then she was asked and who is with you and she replied "I'm all alone, I'm by myself." and with a sigh the attendant said "No one can enter here alone." and so we need to tell everybody about this great Jesus who can redeem us from our sins, the one who died upon the old rugged cross of Calvary for all of us. Maybe this will be a time of recommitment, just think what 12 men did who were really committed to Christ and think what a difference the men who are assembled here and the women who are assembled here could make in the world which we live if all of us would only realize the great potential that is ours and we have this treasure in earthen vessels, but we are to say to anyone we must be impressed with the value of a soul, yonder of man drowning, he sinks beneath the water and you jump in and you going and you save the man and on the shore there is such jubilation because you have given this man 20 years extending his life, 20 years that he would be able to associate with his wife and with his children who otherwise would not have that opportunity but one soul saved in the kingdom of God, we'll live in glory, enjoy equal to the total ages of all who have live from the creation to the end of time, what a great privilege it would be, to be able to say here is my friend that I introduced to Christ.

Look at those that Jesus befriended. Not the upper echelon though he did not certainly disdain them in any way, Nicodemus perhaps on the Sanhedrin the ruler that came to him by night or the Lord did not turn him away and say we need to have you excused because of your place and because of your position but think about those folks, the nobodies, the lonely, the lepers, the cast off, these were the kind of folks that Jesus took time for and so I'm suggesting to you that we need to befriend those just like Jesus befriended the nobodies of his world. He said what man of you having a hundred sheep if one of those goes astray does not leave the ninety and nine and go out into the wilderness to find that which was lost. In the words of Thomas Goodwin, "How glorious did he fulfill his ministry until he had watered every ledge by sea and mountain with his tears, moistened the olive leaves of Gethsemane with the sweat of his brow, and stained his own brow with the blood of his passion, and broke his heart upon a cross of shame." If any man is ashamed to weep over people he is not like the master and so we are to, we are nobody. I'm looking at a bunch of nobodies here, we are nobody and our mission is to tell everybody, that waitress, that person at the grocery store, the garbage people, I'm to tell everybody about somebody, that somebody who was willing to be extended upon the cross of Calvary, six agonizing hours and slowly died for us, to save anyone. I'm convinced that we did not really appreciate the value of a soul. Jesus said "For what shall it profit a man, if he shall gain the whole world, and lose his own soul? Or what shall a man give in exchange for his soul?" Mark 8:36-37.

The soul of man is so valuable. It's valuable because number one of who made it. When I was in high school I went to a private school, Athens Bible School in Athens, Alabama and there was a brother Kirkendall there that taught a course in shop and though my Dad was a general contractor, he owned an insulation company, he never taught me how to saw a board straight. My Dad died at age 56 of a heart attack, 18 months later my mom died and when the children got ready, Dan, my brother and my two sisters got ready to divvy up all of the possessions, lo and behold there was a little stool that I had made in brother Kirkendall's shop. Why in the world did my mom kept this all of those years, was not because it was so artistic or useful, was because of who made it. The Bible says that God "...which stretcheth forth the heavens, and layeth the foundation of the earth, and formeth the spirit of man within him. Zechariah 12:1. The Hebrew writer says "But if ye be without chastisement, whereof all are partakers, then are ye bastards, and not sons. Furthermore we have had fathers of our flesh which corrected us, and we gave them reverence: shall we not much rather be in subjection unto the Father of spirits, and live? For they verily for a few days chastened us after their own pleasure; but he for our profit, that we might be partakers of his holiness. (Hebrews 12:8-10).

He made us and he made everybody living today and then secondly the soul of man is valuable because of how long it's going to last, how old it is. When I was young there was a cup and saucer that I asked my mom when you die can I have it. I knew she must treasure it because she always tried to keep it in a special place and sure enough when my mom died the children said did she promise this to you. 4-5 years ago I got a call from somebody, they said do you have the old cup and saucer that used to belong to your mom and I said yes, we'd like to come and look at it. They came over they looked at that thing, they took pictures of that cup and that saucer, they took pictures of me holding it, they took pictures of it by itself, they said how much would you take for it? They seem to think that that was a very valuable cup, they had even trace the history of it was given by a man before the Civil War to his bride, it's an old, old item, it's not for sale because it belong to somebody that I love very much and some of my children have already asked for it, so I don't guess it'll be for sale later on. Some things are valuable because of their age, you realize a soul of man is eternal; it's forever and then the cost that was paid. The soul of man is so valuable because of what it cost, what do things cost us.

Mrs. Fleming moved close to us on 6th Avenue there in Jasper and I remember the occasion when she he came down and asked my mom in the fall of the year I'm going to take my four children out to pick cotton this year would you like for me to take yours? And for the first time I went out on a cotton patch it was not all bad because she had a daughter that I was a little bit interested in but that girl could pick 200 pounds and I had trouble picking even 100 pounds, at the end of that fall, discounting the dollars of the moon pies, I had enough to buy me a suit. I think it cost from JC Penney something like $27. I've had people give me suits that been worth a lot more than that. I remember not long ago a brother came to me and said that I like for you to go with me, I said where you want to go, I'd like for you to go with me to the clothing store. Well I don't really need to go, I want you to help me pick out a suit and so I thought well he's an aged man and I'll go over and help pick out a suit and we got over to that store and lo and behold that brother said this is my preacher and I want you to get him a suit to wear and I remember that you know I went to the $100 - $150 and you said no, no, I want the finest suit in this store that you have. Well I've had some suits that were more expensive but never a suit like that old suit that I earned that fall. The soul of man cost the precious blood of Jesus. We were redeemed not with corruptible things such as silver and gold from our vain conversation which we've received by tradition but by the precious blood of Jesus Christ, as a lamb without blemish and without spot and so here is somebody that is a nobody. Here is a somebody that you know you're in a hurry, you don't want to get involved in their life but here is somebody for whom our blessed Savior died. May God help us that we may realize the value of the work in which were involved, may we never be a professional. We are going to get paid, but may we never preach for the money. May we never teach the Bible for the money that we're receiving, may we be amateurs, may we be the folks that serve God just for the love of it. Let us close in prayer.

Father for thy blessings we give thanks, we're grateful father for these men who teach your word on a regular basis, we're aware father that even those who have assembled here could make such an impact on the world for years and years to come. We pray father that you would help us not to be professionals, help us father just to be simple amateurs to realize the value of even one soul and to do everything within our power, to reach another before it is everlastingly too late. Thank you Father for this program, thank you for the churches that permit men to come and for those that encourage, thank you that we could be here this afternoon, in the name of Jesus we pray, Amen.

EVANGELISM
JESUS STYLE

The month of July has been the month in which we have been trying to give emphasis to evangelism and we presented last week a lesson about how I can most effectively serve God. The lesson next Sunday morning will also be in this same vane as we talk about it. Today, I want to speak just a few moments concerning evangelism Jesus style. I hope you will study along with us. The text that was read tells us about how a certain man who was a king made a marriage feast for his son and he went out and invited folks to come. They had already received their wedding invitation but they did not show up. Toward the end of that setting when the king heard about what had happened, he was angry. He sent forth his army and destroyed those murderers and burned up their cities. Then he said to his servants the wedding is ready but they which were bidden were not worthy. Go ye therefore in the highways and as many as ye shall find, bid to the marriage. Today I want to speak to you about what I believe is one of the most neglected commandments of all of God's word. Today I speak to you on what may be the Christian's greatest fear. If you would say what is the greatest fear that I have, I am sure this would rank very high. That is personal evangelism—the sharing of one's faith with someone else. God does not expect us to do what we cannot do.

God does not expect a person that has no teeth to brush their natural teeth. God does not expect a bald headed man to comb his hair, but God does expect us to do what we can. The scriptures tell us that we are to tell others the message that we have received. In Matthew chapter 28, Jesus says to his apostles, eleven of them were present when he gave this great commission. "Go ye therefore and teach all nations baptizing them in the name of the Father, the Son, and the Holy Ghost."

He said,"Teaching them to observe all things whatsoever I have commanded you." So here is the unending cycle of Christianity. We are to teach and we have taught we are to baptize folks in the name of the Father, Son, and Holy Ghost. Then we are to teach them to observe all things of whatever the Lord has commanded. In Mark 16:15, he said go ye in to all the world and preach the gospel to every creature. In Luke 24:46, he said, "Thus it is written, and thus it behooved the Christ, the suffering to rise from the dead the third day that repentance and remission of sins should be preached among all nations beginning at Jerusalem."

Now I have a question as we begin our lesson today. How do you feel about personal evangelism? I don't want to be mean spirited today. I don't want to be ugly, but I would like for us to take a little survey this morning.

Questions:

1) How many people have I helped lead to Christ? Maybe you helped by giving an invitation to a service. Maybe you helped by knocking on some door. May be you encouraged some relative to study the Bible or come to a Bible class. The question is how many people have I helped lead to Christ? I wonder what number you would put that in that particular slot today.

2) How many people do I now have in my heart set on to win to Christ? If I asked you today for a list, please get out your list of those you are trying to lead to Christ. Would it be possible that I am speaking to some of us today that have zero on our list? We don't have a list in our billfold or purse. We don't have a list even in our mind of those we are endeavoring

to lead to Christ. I would like for you to please tell me how we are carrying out the commission that God gave every Christian to evangelize the world and to teach those that are lost about the gospel of Christ.

3) Approximately how many hours or minutes per week do I average talking to people about the Lord? I know you talk to them about football, baseball, and cooking. I know that you talk to your friends and neighbors about many subjects. Here is the issue this morning and that is how many hours or minutes do I speak per week talking to people about the Lord. Would you be honest this morning and say, you know I am afraid I can't remember a single soul that I talked to in the last month and I am ashamed of that. We need to repent this morning because we are not carrying out the commission. Oh we will come and take the Lord's supper, sing, give money when the collection basket comes by but here ladies and gentleman and beloved brethren here is that which has authorized us to do and that is tell others about his message of redemption.

4) Do I pray fervently that I might become a better soul winner? Am I praying that God will help me to be a better soul winner.

5) Do you think you have become a soul winner until you try? May I ask that question again. Do you think you will ever become a soul winner until you try?

6) When do I plan to begin? Well if you haven't already started please write in the word, today. Today would be a great day wouldn't it? Today would be a wonderful day for me to talk to others about the Lord. Now the Lord does not expect me to

do what I cannot do but the Lord does expect me to do what I can do. Please remember, God knows what I really can do and what I cannot do and I cannot deceive God. I will be responsible for not making some attempt. I am commissioned to do what I can, not what I cannot do, but what I can do.

In a survey that was recently given and I have seen this survey many, many times but it continues about the same numbers. The average church baptizes about 5% of its membership annually. That is about what we do here, about 5%. We think we are really doing great if we baptize 40 or 50 a year with 800-900 members. That would be about that number, 5%. If you take away the children, that number comes to about 2%. So it takes 98% of us to evangelize those that we are teaching the gospel of Christ. Now we cannot always measure true success by the people we bring up in the baptistry. Noah for example, all of us would say Noah was a great servant of God, but Noah preached for more than 100 years and when he calculated those he had led to God there were only 8 including himself. Jeremiah preached for more than 40 years. Jeremiah, how did you do, how many people did you lead to God. Jeremiah would have to say I don't know a single person. You mean zero? That is exactly what I am saying. Well Jeremiah why didn't you get discouraged? Why didn't you quit? Why didn't you say let somebody else do it? Because God had told me to be that sounding voice to those who might have the opportunity to turn to him. Ezekiel, how many did you turn to God? Ezekiel would also have to say as far as I know not a single one did I ever lead to Christ. Well, beloved that shows us that God is not interested in the number, he is interested in the effort that we put forth. Isaiah said so shall my word be that goeth forth out of my mouth, it shall not return unto me void. That is God making a promise. When he said when my servant, when that word goes from the mouth of my servant that word will not return to me void but it shall accomplish that which I please and it shall prosper in the things where to I sent it. This is a promise that God makes to all of us. In 1 Corinthians 3:6, Paul said I have planted, Apollos watered but God gave the increase. Our job is to do the planting. Our job is to water and then it will be God who will promise, and he makes that promise to us, that I will give the increase.

What would you say is the greatest need in the church today is? What really is the greatest need that we have in the church today. Do we need more luxurious buildings? Do we need more fine commodious, beautiful buildings? Is that the greatest need in the church of our Lord today? Do we need more buses? What is the greatest need today? Do we need more benevolent money helping those that are in need? Well there is more to the game than just planning a play in the huddle.

In an editorial quite a number of years ago, brother Rule Inman wrote the following: He said lets get out of the huddle. A few days ago, brother Lemon said, we were watching a great game on television. There was fierce competition and the score was close. Time was running out and the team that was ahead was in the huddle. They stayed there, and stayed, and stayed and they stayed. The referee blew his whistle and he penalized the team for delaying the game. They had stayed too long in the huddle. Now huddles are absolutely necessary but games are not won in the huddle. They are won on the line. Strategies set are important but we can stay in the huddle too long. Many an important piece of work is discussed in the elder meetings and it is postponed until the next meeting. The next meeting we discuss the same old thing again. I am ashamed to tell you and I have been attending meetings for more than 50 years but I am ashamed to tell you that many, many hours are spent wasting time in the huddle. We talk about things only to talk about them again next week, and next week, and next week. We look at the agenda and how long are we going to stay in the huddle. Beloved brethren, elders should realize that the great referee may severely penalize them for staying in the huddle too long. The congregation can do the same thing. They huddle every Sunday. They leave the huddle to rehuddle next Sunday. They never manage to get down on the line of scrimmage. In fact, the whole church is gaining a world wide reputation for huddling. We flock to ourselves, we talk to ourselves, we huddle with our heads down around the Lord's table and some of teams are even careless about making the huddle. Some of our team members don't even show up for the huddle but worship is essential. Worship is important but only if it inspires us to get out and do something and that something is to share the message of redemption with somebody else. Brethren do you think you are doing all that God wants you to do when you are in the huddle? You are not going to win the game in the huddle and we are not going to evangelize to our community in the huddle. We need to get out on the line. The enemy has rolled back, not from the huddle but from the line of scrimmage. It takes all the effort every individual is capable of putting forth in order to win. Are we concerned about trying to be what our master was? His goal and his purpose was to seek and to save the lost. If we are imitators of Christ why is that not our goal today? If we want to be like our master as Paul commanded us that we are to be imitators of him even as he was of Christ. Why don't we get out of the huddle and teach the lost and rapidly inspire the world?

Instead we would rather huddle back on the line of scrimmage and just talk about the battle and sit down and open the book on somebody's kitchen table is what we need to be doing and quoting this saith the Lord to them. One gospel meeting that we hold here at Roebuck Parkway is not carrying out the commission that God has given to all of us. It will just not get the job done. I am all in favor of a gospel meeting. I want us to knock on those 12,000 doors that we set our goal to knock on. That is doing far more than a lot of other churches are doing but I am saying to you we need to do more than just a 1 month 1 week out of the 52 weeks effort to evangelize the world in which we live. The greatest need today is for the church to get back on the mission that God has assigned. In Luke 19:10 the Bible says, the Son of man has come to seek and to save that which was lost. God could have done anything he wanted to do with Jesus but he made him a soul winner. We have many capable workers in the huddle but we definitely need personal workers out in the field. In Luke chapter 1, after these things the Lord appointed other 70 also and he sent them to and to before his face into every city and place whether he himself would come. Therefore he said unto them, the harvest truly is great but the laborers are few. Pray ye therefore for the Lord of harvest that he will send forth laborers into the vineyard. Christ needs you. Not Uncle Sam needs you beloved but Christ needs you. He is the head. We are the feet. We are his voice. We are his hands. The Lord needs us. We are to be the salt of the earth. Matthew 5:13, ye are the salt of the earth and salt preservers. We cannot preserve sitting on the shelf. We have to rub that salt into the meat. We have to put that salt where the salt is intended to be preserved and so it is with us. We need genuine concern for those that are lost. Paul said I say the truth in Christ. I lie not. My conscience also bearing witness in the Holy Ghost that I have great heaviness and continued sorrow in my heart where I could wish that myself were accursed from Christ for my brethren, my kinsman according to the flesh. Paul what keeps you going on and on and telling others about the message of redemption. Why is it that you cannot rest?

Why is that you spend every night and every day sharing the message with somebody else? Because I recognize that those that are not taught the gospel are lost. If everyone had a terminal illness and you had found the cure for that illness, would you share it or would you keep it for yourself? Beloved, we have the treasure. We have the message of redemption and we must not selfishly keep it.

Reasons that we need to do personal work, I want to just simply list the few reasons that I am convinced that all of us here. Remember, God doesn't just want you to do what you can't do but God does want you to do everything you can do. If you can invite that person that checks out the grocery. If you can invite that person when you go in to the service station. God expects us to do what we can do and that is all that God expects us to do but he does expect us to do that. We need to constantly keep that on our minds. I believe one of the big reasons we are not more evangelistic is that we get sidetracked and unconcerned about those that are our friends and neighbors who know not the message of redemption. Here are some reasons that we need to be personal workers.

1) It is a direct command from God. The text that we read in Matthew 20:20, he said that we are to go and to teach all nations. Then he says Lord I am with you always even to the end of the world that we are to teach those that have been taught. We would not forsake the Lord's supper. There are people in this assembly today that have not missed the Lord's Supper in the last 10 years. We would not lie. There are those of us that would rather have our tongues cut out as to lie. We would not steal. We don't go down to Walmart or down to some store and see how much we can take out of that store yet we ignore the injunction where it says we are to go and to teach those the gospel. This is the great commission. This is not the great omission. This is the great commission, we are to go and we are to evangelize the world.

2) It is necessary for our self preservation. In Luke chapter 13, Jesus told this parable. He said a certain man had a fig tree planted in his vineyard. He came and sought fruit thereon and found none. He said to the dresser of the vineyard. Behold these 3 years I come seeking fruit on this fig tree and I find none. Cut it down. Why cumberith the ground? He answered and said unto him, Lord let it alone. This year also til I shall dig about it and dung it and if it bear fruit well and if not then after that thou shalt cut it down. So what is the Lord going to do for us?

The fruit of the Christian, one of the fruits is another Christian. How long has it been since we have borne fruit for our master. If an employee does not do his job right would you keep him around? If we do not teach, the blood is going to be upon our hands. In Acts 18:6, and when they opposed themselves and blasphemed he shook his raiment and said unto them your blood be upon your own head. I am clean from henceforth I will go to the gentiles. Can we say the same thing to our neighbors and to our friends. Can we say, I have done everything I know to do to encourage you to become a Christian and to have opportunity to study the Bible with you and your blood be upon your own hands. But look at Ezekiel, when I say to the wicked, thou shalt surely die and I giveth him not warning nor speak to warn the wicked from his wicked ways to save his life. The same wicked man shall die in his iniquity but his blood will I require at thine hands. Brethren that is one of the scariest verses in all of the Bible. He says you are exempt from any responsibility if you had made that effort and attempt to warn the wicked of his wicked way. If you remain silent and do nothing at all to win him to Christ, he said his blood I am going to require at your hands.

3) We need to be like the early Christians. In Acts chapter 8:4, "Therefore they that were scattered abroad went everywhere preaching the word of God." The word preaching here is not kairos, but it is the word ugondolista which simply means they went everywhere teaching the word of God, both men and women. In Acts 26:20, but I showed first unto them of Damascus and Jerusalem and through all the coast of Judea then to the gentiles they should repent and turn to God and do works meet for repentance. We should do that to be like the early church. We are not like the early church. We may have the right name. We may have the right kind of worship but beloved unless we are sharing the message with others we are not like the early New Testament church.

4) Because I am a debtor. Paul said in Romans 1:14, "I am a debtor both to the Greek and the barbarian, both to the wise and unwise." Paul have you borrowed some money? No but I have the message of salvation and as long as I have that message of redemption, I have an obligation to share it with others. Then I would say because of the joy of being a soul winner. It gives joy first of all to the heavenly Father. In Luke 15:7, "I say unto you that likewise joy shall be in heaven over one sinner that repenteth more than over 90 and 9 just who need no repentance." Who is going to rejoice when that sinner comes down the isle. When we following a Bible class encourage them to obey. It is going to be God the Father who rejoices. There is joy in the presence of the angels. Maybe the angels are happy too, but I believe in the presence of the angels refers to that father when that prodigal son came back home. You think that father's heart was glad or sad? You know he was thrilled. Then secondly, there is that personal joy. In Philippians 4:1, therefore my dearly beloved and long for my joy, my crown so stand fast in the Lord my dearly beloved. Look at Paul's attitude toward those who he had been responsible for their conversion. In 3 John 4, he says I have no greater joy than to hear that my children walk in the truth.

There is more to the game then just staying in the huddle. What I am saying to us today is we need to get out of the huddle. Why beloved we could encourage people to come, invite them to come to services, and if you invite a 100 people and everyone of them say I am not interested and tell you to get lost and go peddle your papers somewhere else at least we have done the will of God. We have done what God told us to do but as long as we are smug and content to observe the communion, sing praises to His name, and bow our head at the appropriate time and we don't get off of these pews and have any concern for our friends and neighbors that are lost, we are failing in the mission that God has assigned to us.

You think I am mad at you? I am not angry. I just want us to realize that this is a message from God. This is what God has instructed to us. All of us need to do this. We have different degrees. I believe God expects more out of brother Kyle than he does out of somebody that may be doesn't have as much ability but God expects us to use whatever abilities we may have to His glory and to the advancement of his kingdom. Just think what we could be if we would carry forth the commission that God has assigned to us. I am grateful that it has been suggested that we spend the month of July talking on the subject of evangelism. I know it is an old subject. I know it is so preached about that maybe at times it might have even become trite and meaningless to us but beloved it is the message from God.

If you are here today and you are not a member of the Lord's church you want to become a Christian. You ask what must I do. First of all, you must be willing to hear Jesus, not hear what this preacher says or what some man or woman may say but be willing to listen to Jesus. God tells you to believe in his son. The word believes simply means to trust. Do you trust Jesus? Jesus said it in John 8:24, "Except you believe I am He, ye shall die in your sins." Thirdly, he tells us to repent.

Repentance is a change of mind that will bring about a change of action. Luke 13:3, "I tell you nay but except you repent you shall all likewise perish." Romans 10:10, the Bible says, "With the mouth confession is made unto salvation." Then we are to be immersed into the waters of baptism for the remission of sins. It is in this action that we are baptized into Christ. We come in contact with the shed blood of Jesus and we are added to his family. Jesus says he that believeth and is baptized shall be saved. Baptism and salvation, baptism never follows salvation. In every passage where they are mentioned together from cover to cover in this book the Bible shows us that we are baptized before we are saved. We are baptized in order to be forgiven of our sins and this is exactly the message we need to proclaim. If you are here today and you haven't been faithful. May be you have not been a soul winner please pray that God would forgive you personally because I do not know who is a soul winner and who is not. There is no reason for you to come forward this morning. We don't say you are doing wrong by coming forward but I believe our resolve needs to be within our own heart. You may be sitting today next to your wife or your husband and you may make that commitment. I am going to be a soul winner for Jesus. I have been convinced Lord from your word that you want me to do what I can to share this message with others. Will you repent for your past faith and will you acknowledge it from now on from this day forward that you are going to be a soul winner for the master. If you need to respond publicly and you desire the prayers of the congregation we urge you to come. Will you come now as together we stand as we sing.

THE NEED FOR
DEDICATION

One of Dad's most often preached sermons was titled: The Need for Dedication. It moved both of us. We both have preached this sermon many times. In fact, Dale was so struck by it that he used it as his "tryout sermon" for a number of years. The notes below are his (Dale's) notes on that sermon:

J & D

What does the church need? Better programs, more money, young couples, nice buildings, influential people, good elders, better preaching? All of those might be...but the need of the hour is for saints dedicated totally and completely to God.

(Cartoon) "Going up hill sure is fun, if up hill is where you want to be." Being a Christian is fun, if doing right is really what you want to do.

I. I hope in this lesson to stir us to see the need for more dedication.

Christianity is not a glorified hayride.

It is not a satisfied picnic.

It is not a social club.

Christianity is a vineyard looking for workers.

Christianity is a battlefield looking for soldiers.

Christianity is a race looking for racers.

The word: Dedicate occurs 4 times, Dedicating 22 times, Dedicated 2 times, Dedication 10 times. So in all its forms the word is found some 38 times in the New Testament

16 Items are said to be dedicated:

The Temple, Items in the Temple, Spoils from battle Gifts, Children, Animals, Walls of Jerusalem, Nebuchadnezzar's idol

Dedication the word in the Greek means

1. New in quality. Like you take an old car and restore it. Like in Hebrews 9:18 that indicates that the first covenant was dedicated with blood.

2. New in time As in Hebrews 10:20 new as opposed to old! A new covenant.

Webster says the word means "to set apart or consecrate to a divine being. Give wholly to." There are other words kin to it like: "Consecrate"- 41 times and "Devote"- 9 times

In more recent times the ideal has been changed. Some have gone too far—set up own laws-Confession to a prayer partner, like w/the Crossroads movement of a few years ago. But don't throw the baby out with the bath water. Don't throw away the ideal of being totally and wholly committed to our Master.

Some say, "God has no right." "No one is going to tell me how to live." What is the basis of dedication?

II. I submit to you that God has a right to expect dedication of us:

First of all because He created us In Genesis 1:1 "In the beginning God created the heavens and the earth." (Gen 2:7 KJV) "And the LORD God formed man of the dust of the ground, and breathed into his nostrils the breath of life; and man became a living soul." In John 1 beginning with verse 1: "In the beginning was the Word, and the Word was with God, and the Word was God. {2} The same was in the beginning with God. {3} All things were made by him; and without him was not any thing made that was made." So God made us.

Not only that but He sustains us Heb 1:3 "He upholds all things by the word of His power." And in Acts 17:25 "...he giveth to all life, and breath, and all things;" The present tense is employed meaning, He keeps on giving.

A man once was a great artist. He had drawn many wonderful paintings but destitute times arose and he was forced to sell his cherished items one by one. He was down only to one painting and with great reluctance he sold that final painting. Several years later, prosperity was again his and he saw this beautiful painting on sale at an auction. He was overjoyed. He bid on his own painting and when the hammer was rung down on item, he walked out with his own painting. He patted the painting and said: "Twice mine. Twice mine". That's the way we are with God. We are twice God's. Once because of creation. We are also God's because of redemption. We have been bought back. (1 Pet 1:18-19 KJV) "Forasmuch as ye know that ye were not redeemed with corruptible things, as silver and gold, from your vain conversation received by tradition from your fathers; {19} But with the precious blood of Christ, as of a lamb without blemish and without spot:"

As we think about the basis for dedication. Not only for these three reasons Not only 1-3 but more than this because we have voluntarily devoted our lives to His service. Every child of God has given himself to God. (1 Cor 6:19-20 NKJV) "...you are not your own? {20} For you were bought at a price; therefore glorify God in your body and in your spirit, which are God's.

And things devoted to God must not be misappropriated. O.T.

In Joshua 6:19 all the silver, gold, iron are dedicated to the Lord, they shall come unto the treasury of the Lord." As they were entering into the land of promise, about to do battle with Jericho. And God sounded out this warning—"These things are mine. They've been dedicated to me. I own them." No wonder then, when we read of Akin taking a Babylonish garrment, 200 pieces of silver 50 shekels of gold. No wonder God was displeased! These things belonged to God. Look at the punishment!

Lev. 25:23—"The land is mine." God said, "I own the land, it's been dedicated to me, therefore you are not to sell it." No wonder when Naboth was approached by Ahab to buy his land so that Ahab could plant a better garden near his palace, Naboth said I cannot sell the garden, it has been dedicated to God! I cannot not use it just any way I wish.

20 times in the Bible the 7th is called Gods. A man violated Sabbath-Numbers 15:35. Stone Him! What was God's had been misused.

Malachi 3:8—Will a man rob God? Yet you have been robbing me. And you say, how have we been robbing you. In tithes and offerings. Malachi 1:14—It's God's—NO right to misuse them.

Now we have a need to be dedicated.

First of all we have a need to be dedicated in order to please God—1 Cor. 6; Mt. 16:24; (Luke 9:23 NKJV) "...If anyone desires to come after Me, let him deny himself, and take up his cross daily, and follow Me.

You have two choices:

One says follow Christ—lose your life for his sake/forsake world/his reward.

One says follow the World—Grab all the gusto you can. world/ condemn!

In Romans 12:1 Paul said (Rom 12:1 KJV) "I beseech you therefore, brethren, by the mercies of God, that ye present your bodies a living sacrifice, holy, acceptable unto God, which is your reasonable service."

Just as that land was dedicated to God and he owned it. Same with us. We belong to God! Sometimes somebody will say "It's my own life let me live as I want! "No" God says, "I made you, reconciled you & I sustain you!" You're his.Lk 9:23

Speech—1 billion curse said daily. I do not have a right to just talk anyway I want to talk. Dress, actions, how you spend your time.

Do's—no—voluntary.

There are 4 therefore's in Romans:

> Romans 3:20—the "Therefore" of condemnation
> Romans 5:1—Justification
> Romans 8:1—Assurance
> Romans 12:1—Dedication

III. Christian dedication requires 3 things:

Giving of our bodies

Romans 12:1—"present your bodies a living sacrifice.
6:1—God forbid! How—continue—No!
6:16—Shall we commit sin—sin—No!
Romans 6 he tells us the four new things we have: freedom,
fellowship, fruits (we are those!), future

There are 2 living sacrifices in the Bible worthy of note:

Gen. 22—Isaac yielded himself
Jesus—A willing sacrifice bearing our wounds.

"Present"—once for all time! Not something done half-heartedly.
Not holding on to God with one hand. But a once a for all
giving.

Giving of our minds! I come find your Bible here.—From a study
of God's word.

Giving of our will—by daily commitment.—Costs!

Why be dedicated?

Because God wants this- we are commanded. We want
spirituality without sacrifice —we want easy Christianity —we
want to be close to God but we want Him to stoop down not us
to stretch up —we'll never get it. There are no easy crosses to
bear..

It beautifies the gospel: A man opposed to worship—wife! He
slapped her and said "I don't want you to go". Gun—"if you pull

the trigger I'm going to heaven. If you don't I'm going to church." Now that's the kind of dedication that God wants.

My great grandfather was a gospel preacher—30 years old when he became a Christian—50 years a preacher. Many think he's the backbone of our family. Our family has a number of gospel preachers.

90 years young—A little lady who has stood like the rock of Gibraltar. Who said "It doesn't matter what it cost you must do what's right."

She married at 15 a non-Christian. He made it hard for her so she stopped attending. One night a friend invited her to a Gospel Meeting she went "I'm going to be dedicated!"

Cut a switch hit children. Crying for mother. "I didn't get much out of the service that night." All lanterns cut off. She said, "Authur, I'm, going to get the constable."

Next day—He was out plowing and she went to where he was and said "you may kill me and you may kill the children but I'm never going to put you before the Lord again." Years went by and one day he started getting ready—stood outside was baptized. When the song started he came down the aisle.

What lead him to the Lord!

The power of a gospel preacher—NO—dedicated Christian woman. How many have given up, what's the use? The cost is too great Too much at stake.

Dedication beautifies the gospel.

Many of us here today have been Christians for a long time. We'd all have to admit at times it gets discouraging. And I thought we could re-inforce the lesson by looking at the life of one really dedicated to God.

IV. I think we find something in Jeremiah.

He was called when he was real young. Jeremiah 1—I am but a youth. Paul said let no man despise they youth. But Jeremiah was despising his own youth.

He was faithful because he believed in doing right—He persevered because he was dedicated. But it wasn't easy

Unusual Commandments

God gave Jeremiah some unusual commandments I don't want us to just look at these for the facts but for how they might affect our lives. Jer. 16:1—Don't get married. God gave Abraham a difficult commandment-sacrifice your son. God given us some.

Love our enemy and brethren. Sometimes it easier to love my enemies than some ole' brother who is cantankerous. I've never met an elder or preacher who didn't have to work on this very thing. Let's someone who complains and gripes about everything-what am I going to do? Love him. And that ole' brother who comes out with a note-you mispronounced this word, or you were wrong about this, or who drums up others to oppose you and you know he's after you. What will we do with those we just can't please?

People who have been here since day one stand (first three months). People who have placed membership in last three months stand...talk to both groups —long timers —tired, "be not weary..." "having begun..." Newbies..great stuff, no vetting,

Give what he wants. Boy! Worm; cooked; set! I want Dad to eat ½ of it. You ate the wrong ½. Someone you just can't please. I am to love them, pray for them.

Jeremiah had a right. But he kept on preaching.

Forgive - Matthew 18

Lonely Commandment

Waistcloth bury it—spoiled Visual aid.

Potter's house—jar That's the way Israel is.

He didn't quit! He was totally committed.

They hated him. They put him in a pit. Beat him. It's not always popular to do right! But look to Jeremiah. Godly people have often been lonely at times—Daniel, Jesus; Noah; at school, work. Have you ever been lonely as you tried to do right?

Sorrowful Commandment

Jeremiah 9:1-4 I could wish my eyes were like fountains. We need to be happy! But he also said Blessed are they that mourn.

The tears of the prophet—Lamentations. As he mourned his city.

We too, have stood a begged for one to do right. And had deep sorrow when they didn't.

Wearisome Commandment

Dedication will bring you back. More than 40 years Jeremiah preached—"You're not going to be successful." Before you get started. Why? Because God has always given men opportunities to repent. Elders, teachers, servants, God didn't promise our success here. Ours the same.

T.B. Larimore tells the story of coming home at dark and he told his momma-he said it's dark and I'm afraid. For the rest of that time his mom met him with a lantern...Do you believe your mom will be waiting? I don't know, but I do know my Lord will be there.

Matthew 13:44-for joy. I'll do things for my Lord...

SAVING FAITH

Meetings—Dad loved preaching Gospel Meetings. Like most preachers who preach a lot of Gospel Meetings Dad had his staple sermons. For many years this sermon or a version of it was one of those.

Back in 1963 a young Jerry Jenkins was invited to speak at Pepperdine in California (that lecture is in this book). He was on the program with Gus Nichols. As he told the story he drove from Hamilton, AL and met up with Brother Nichols in Jasper. From there they drove old Highway 78 to Birmingham. Somewhere along the way Dad asked Brother Nichols to help him in understanding faith and grace and works and how they work together. Brother Nichols began to talk and Dad took notes, writing as fast as he could. They got to the airport and to the gate. Brother Gus continued to talk and Dad continued to write. At some point Dad started a new yellow legal pad. Once on the long plane ride the pattern continued. At some point Brother Nichols said to Dad: "Son, looks like you are getting tired" and took the notebook and continued to write the rest of the flight. Dad kept those notes on Faith and used the sermons from that conversation the rest of his life.

Another quick Gospel Meeting sermon. As we said back a few chapters ago: Dad was a soul winner. He was known to invite someone he had a study going with to go with him one night of a meeting. If they went, it didn't matter what topic or text he had been assigned. He would preach an evangelistic sermon straight to the heart of the person with whom he was studying.

J & D

Thank you very much for coming and being with us this evening. This is a wonderful Monday night attendance. We appreciate this so very much as already has been so ably indicated. Those of you who are visiting with us at our service tonight. It is difficult at times preaching gospel meetings in our culture today because it seems that fewer and fewer people are involved. I suppose that is because we have such local men, not like it was quite a number of years ago when they did not have a local preacher. So, when the preacher would come around, the folks would flock in, but I know there are many places that you could have gone this evening. We are very grateful you are here with us. I am really surprised at what a marvelous job your song leader did tonight. I sat by him at supper and I did not think he could do it, but he survived. I do appreciate the wonderful song service. I had some meetings this year where the song leaders did not carry a tune in a bucket. It really detracts from a gospel meeting. You have a great blessing here to have such a capable man to direct your song service at these gospel services. Also, I would be remiss if I failed to express sincere appreciation to the ladies who prepared such a marvelous meal. Yesterday, I got tricked. I went into the kitchen and thought that was all the food that was here. I went on into the next room and low and behold there was a line of tables there with food all over the place. This is an eating congregation. I appreciate so much the wonderful, sweet fellowship that we have.

1. Yesterday, we talked primarily to the church about a very elementary lesson concerning a subject that is very vital. I am convinced that we never need to depart from God's will and God's word. The Bible has a great deal to say about the topic that we are to study about tonight. We are always to be students

of the word. Hosea 4: 6 "My people are destroyed for lack of knowledge." John 8: 31-32 "Jesus said if you continue at My word, you are My disciples indeed and you shall know the truth. The truth shall make you free." Ephesians 5:17 "Be not unwise, understanding what the will of the Lord is." 2nd Timothy 2:15 "Study to show thyself approved of the God, workmen needeth not to be ashamed, rightly dividing the word of truth. 1 Peter 3:15 "But sanctify the Lord God in your heart. Be ready always to give an answer to every man that ask of the reason of the hope within you, yet with meekness and with fear." The Bible repeats scriptures that inform us that we are to be students of His holy will. We are always to study His word. We are never to take anything for granted when it comes to the will of God. Thereby, we need to be constant students of that word. We do not ever need to think that we have arrived and no longer need to read and to study the will of God. That is a fair idea indeed and certainly it should not characterize the people of God today. The Bible indicates there are activities, in which salvation is essential. There is activity that we must do in order to be saved. Titus 2:11-12 "The grace of God that brings us salvation has appeared unto all men, teaching us that denying ungodliness and worldly lusts." We should live soberly, righteously and godly in this present world. The grace of God brings salvation, has appeared to all men and yet not all men are going to be saved. You know we live in a world of faith. I think about that sometimes. When you drive down the highway, maybe a two lane road and you are driving maybe 55-65 mph. Just a few feet away from you there is another car coming in the opposite direction. Occasionally, someone gets over on the lane too far.

SERMONS OF JERRY A. JENKINS - 73

Think about the faith that is involved simply in driving an automobile. We live in a world of faith, don't we? We have faith in our mail system. We may not always like what we have in the system, but we have faith in it. There are billions of people that live upon the face of the earth, but if you have the name and address, you can send a letter to anybody in the world today. Isn't that marvelous? How great that is. By faith we write a letter, we seal it up in an envelope, we put an address outside, we take it down and put it in a blue and red box. We also believe that someone is going to come there and take that letter to send it somewhere. We live in a world of faith. Somebody said I do not have faith in anything, well we do live in a world of faith. I know sometimes our faith is not where it actually ought to be. My grandfather, John, had a great deal of faith in a product called oil of Saul I do not know whether any of you have heard of oil of Saul or not, but my grandfather thought that would cure about anything. I have heard him say that if you cut a dog's tail off and you put a little oil of Saul on that dog, it would grow a new tail. It was a marvelous thing. Then he said, if you put Saul on that cut off dog's tail it would grow a new dog. I mean, he believed in that. I think his faith was a little misappropriated and misput, but I am suggesting to you today that we live in a world of faith. The Bible indicates that we are saved by faith. In John 3:16, the passage you have known most of your life, "For God so loved the world that He gave His only begotten Son, that whosoever believes in Him shall not perish, but have everlasting life." John 3:18 "He that believeth is not condemned, but he that believeth not is condemned already because he has not believed in Jesus the Lord, the Son of God." In John 3:38 the scriptures indicate that we are saved, or our salvation, depends upon our faith. In John 5:24 Jesus said,

"Verily, verily I say unto you, he that heareth My word and believeth on Him that has sent Me hath everlasting life and shall not come to condemnation, but is passed from death unto life." In Acts 16:31 "Believe on the Lord Jesus Christ and thou shall be saved and thy house." The Bible teaches that we are saved by faith. We must believe in Jesus to be saved. In Romans 5:1 "Therefore, being justified by faith, we have peace with God through our Lord Jesus Christ." The word justified means just as if I never committed a sin. The Bible says we are justified by faith. These are but a few scriptures in the holy will of God that indicate to us that we are saved by faith. We are justified by faith. We are redeemed by faith. So, we cannot have any dispute tonight over the fact that the Bible teaches that we are redeemed and saved by our faith in the Lord Jesus Christ. We ought not to be afraid to just come out and say it. We are saved by faith. The Bible again and again reaffirms we are saved by faith. There are passages that indicate the responsibility that man has. In Luke 6:46 Jesus said, "Why do you call me Lord, Lord and do not the things that I say?" In Matthew 7, not everyone that says unto Me, Lord, Lord, shall enter the kingdom of Heaven, but he that does the will of my Father, which is in Heaven. In James 1:21 "Wherefore lay apart all filthiness and superfluity of naughtiness, and receive with meekness the engrafted word." Be you doers of the Word and not just ears only, deceiving your own selves. James 1:25 "Whosoever looketh into the perfect law of liberty and continueth therein, he being not a forgetful hearer, but a doer of the word. This man should be blessed in this deed." The Bible indicates that there are activities or actions on our part. The Bible uses the word faith in two different ways. The Bible uses the word faith in what we might call the objective manner. By objective faith, we simply mean that body of truth that brings about trust that we have in the Lord. The Bible often uses the word faith as this great body of truth that brings redemption to mankind. For example, in Galatians 1, the past verse of the chapter, they had heard only that Paul was now preaching the faith that he once destroyed. What did Paul preach? He preached the faith. Yet, in Galatians 1:6 Paul said "I marvel that you are so soon removed from Him that called you unto another gospel, which is not another, but there will be some that trouble you and would pervert the gospel of Christ. But tho we, or an angel from Heaven, preach any other gospel unto you than that which we preach, let him be accursed." And so Paul said he preached the gospel, but he said in Galatians 1:23 "He preached the faith. Therefore, the word faith and gospel equal one another. The Bible indicates that Paul preached the faith and preached the gospel. It is said in the book of Acts 6:14 "There were many priests that were obedient to the faith." They were obedient to the gospel of Christ. In Acts 14, we read of how Paul and company came back from missionary journeys and confirmed the brethren. Those that were obedient to the faith. (The word faith here means simply the gospel of the Lord Jesus Christ.) So sometimes, the word faith and gospel refer to the same thing. The word faith is also used in the subjected manner, as in our attitude or trust that we have. Tonight, primarily, we are going to be taking about subjective faith. About that attitude, which brings salvation to us by God's grace and by God's mercy and goodness to us. So we are saved by faith. There can be no doubt about it. We are saved by faith.

I want to raise a question. I want to begin tonight by asking what kind of faith is it that saves us? You know the Bible talks about different types of faith. For example, the Bible said that there was a certain centurion that came to our Lord beseeching that he would heal a trusted servant of his. Evidently, Jesus started toward that man's house. (Matthew 8) It is not necessary for you to go into my room. I am a man of authority, I say that this man go and he go and he goes and another comes and to another, do this and he does it. The Bible says Jesus marveled. You know there are only two times in all the word of God that the Bible says Jesus marveled about anything. It is said of those at Capernaum that he marveled because they did not believe in Him. But, here is a centurion and Jesus marveled. He said, "I have not seen so great of faith, no, not in all of Israel." This man who was a gentile had more faith than Peter, James and John, those who had been with our Lord and had heard him preach. Those that heard him teach the great parables and those who had seen the miracles he had performed. How the lame walked and how the blind were able to see. What a marvelous faith this man must have had. Jesus marveled at this man's faith. Jesus healed his servant. In the same setting, there later in the chapter, there was a certain Syrophoenician woman who had a daughter who was ill. Jesus said, "I am not going to cast the pearls before swine." But this woman said, but Lord even the dogs come and eat the crumbs that fall off the table. Jesus complimented this lady and he said, "Oh great is thy faith." So, the Bible talks about a great faith. What kind of faith saves us? Is it a great faith? But the Bible also talks about little faith. In fact, a number of times in God's word, for example Matthew 14, Jesus was there on the sea of Galilee. They thought he was a ghost. They eventually recognized that it was Jesus. Peter said, if it be you, command that I can come. Peter took a step out on the sea of Galilee. He began to sink and Jesus said, "Oh you of little faith." Several times in God's word, they were rebuked because of their little faith. So we know there is a great faith and there is a little faith. Now, the question is are we saved by little faith? The Bible also talks about weak faith. In Romans 14:1 "Those of you that are weak in the faith, receive you, but not the doubtful disputations." The Bible talks about individuals who have a weak faith. There is also a strong faith. Romans 4:20 "It is said of Abraham that he staggered not at the promise through unbelief, but was strong in faith." So, there is strong faith. There is weak faith. There is great faith. There is little faith. The Bible also speaks of dead faith. James 2:26 "As the body without the spirit is dead. So, faith without works is dead." There is dead faith. Now my question tonight is, what kind of faith saves you? Even the devil believes in God. James 2:19 "You believe there is one God, I do as well." The devil and demons also believe and tremble. In Matthew 8, there was a man possessed with demons. Jesus was about to cast these demons out and they confessed to Him. What are we to do with you Jesus, Son of God? Did you come to torment us before the time? There are those who affirm that man is saved the moment he believes Jesus to be the Son of God. If that be the case, even the demons themselves would be saved. But, the truth of the matter is hell was prepared for the devil and his angels. They are not going to be saved. So, it is possible for individuals to have faith and still not be saved. So, what kind of faith saves us? Brother Guy N. Woods used to tell a story about a man that hollered until he got a group of people together. They threw a rope across a river and waterfall. They asked him if he believed he could walk across that rope. Nobody thought he could do so. He demonstrated. He went across that rope and came back. How many of you believe I can walk across that rope backward? Well a couple raised their hands. They began to believe that this man could maybe do what he said. He demonstrated. He came back and they were amazed. He said how many of you believe I can take this wheel-barrel that has had the tire removed and push this backward and go across that rope. Again, the number grew. Several more raised their hands. They believed he could do so. He demonstrated that. They cheered when he got back. He said how many of you believe I can take this wheel-barrel and walk across this rope, pushing the wheel-barrel in front of me and come back safely. Well, by this time, every hand was raised. They had seen him do that which was more difficult, but now they believed that he could do this. He said who will get in the wheel-barrel and every hand came down. You know, it is possible for us to say we believe in God, to say that we trust in the Lord with all of our hearts until it comes time for our faith to be demonstrated or until it comes time for us to do something that may not seem very logical to us. We do so simply because God has told us to do so. We are like the woman who said she was scared to death when the horses ran away with her. Someone said well, why didn't you trust in the Lord? She said, "I did until the harness broke." Maybe that is the way we are sometimes. I trust in the Lord until it is time for my faith to be demonstrated. So, what kind of faith is it that saves us? It is not the kind of faith that the devils have. They will never repent of their sins. They will never obey the Lord. What kind of faith is it that redeems us from our sins. It is a vibrant, active, obedient and dynamic faith. That is the kind of faith that saves us. We are saved by faith. We do not need to hesitate. Just affirm that we are saved by faith. Then we need to explore what kind of faith it is that saves us. There is another issue that certainly needs to be noticed and that is where does this faith save us?

2. We are saved by faith, but where does this faith save us? Now imagine back here behind me on this screen we took a bucket of red paint and a big ole paintbrush and I drew a great big ole circle there on the canvas. I would raise the question, are we saved inside, the inside of the circle representing our relationship of being in God and in Christ, or are we saved on the outside? Well, the scriptures inform us. In Ephesians 2:11-12 "At that time you were without Christ, being aliens from the commonwealth of Israel, strangers from the covenant of promise having no hope and without God." Those outside that circle, they have no hope and are without God. But, brother Jerry they're good neighbors, good friends and you can always count on them. If they are outside of that circle, the Bible says they have no hope and are without God. We live in a world of hope don't we? I remember when my mom died, several years ago, 1961. I remember the doctor came down and told us that my mother was not going to live. The four of us had gathered at University Hospital in Birmingham. You know, we still had hope. We live in a world of hope. We thought maybe something would be done and some reversal of that old disease called cancer, so that maybe she would live. The doctor said there is no hope.

God says that if you are out of Christ, there is no hope. You may be a good mother. You may be a wonderful grandmother or grandparent. But, if you are outside of that circle where salvation is, then there is no hope. That is what God says in his Holy Word. We can't change it. I have never been to a funeral where the preacher missed a case. If he is going to make any kind of judgement, he always gets them to glory. I heard about one funeral when that did not happen, but I was not in attendance at that funeral. I understand that some of the family members stood up and said well, he knew you taught him, so if he is in hell, you are the reason for it. I was not at that funeral, but I heard about that over in Mississippi several years ago. I have never been to a service where the preacher, if he made any kind of decision about the life that this man lived, he went right on into glory. He went right on into Heaven. But, the Bible says that if you are outside of Christ, there is no hope. I wonder tonight if there is anyone here who is outside of that circle. That is what this meeting is all about. That is why the brethren asked me to preach a little bit on the fundamental lessons because we must not be outside of Christ. What about being inside? The Bible says inside of Christ that we are new creatures (2 Corinthians 5:17.) "If any man be in Christ, he is a new creature. Old things are passed away. Behold all things are become new."

You have a new purpose in life. You have a new dream. You have a new goal in life. One man beat his wife up and after she took it for a while, she left him. She went home to her Daddy. He heard the gospel sermon. He became a new testament Christian. He went to get his wife and her father said, you cannot have her. When you had her, you beat her up. He said I didn't do that, it was the old person. I am a new creature. In Christ we are new creatures. We are new people. We have new goals and aspirations. We do not think and act like we used to. We do not gossip and talk like we used to. We have a new desire and that is to put God first in our life. We attend the services regularly and faithfully. We give of our income. Why? Because we are new creatures in Christ. The Bible also says that forgiveness is in Christ (Ephesians 1:7, Colossians 1:14.) We are new creatures in Christ. The scriptures inform us (2nd Timothy

2:10) that, "salvation is in Christ." We are saved within Christ, not on the outside of Christ, but inside of Christ. In Ephesians 1:3 "Blessed be the God and Father of our Lord Jesus Christ, who has blessed us with all spiritual blessings in heavenly places in Christ."

God makes it rain on the sinner and saint alike. The sunshine grows the crops of the worst infidel you have ever seen. There are some blessings, spiritual blessings like prayer. I know if I were a hardened sinner and things got severe enough, I would call upon God. I understand that principle, but the Bible says the privilege of prayer is to be enjoyed in Christ and not out of Christ. If that is the only reasons you need to obey God tonight, it would be sufficient reason for you to obey His will because God will hear and answer your prayer, in Christ. The peace that passes all understanding is in Christ. The assurance that God is with us. We do not go into that operation room all by ourselves. The Lord is with us if we are in Christ. All who are in Christ experience the blessings of salvation and redemption. What kind of faith saves? It is a faith that humbly submits to God's will. Where does faith save? It saves us in Christ.

3. When are we saved? At what point in our walk with God are we saved? Is it when you attend services the tenth time? Is that when you are saved? Is it when you give a certain amount of money that you are saved? When are we saved. We are not saved at the moment that we believe. The Bible indicates numerous examples of those that believed and they were outside of Christ. John 12:48-49 "Nevertheless, among the chief rulers, many believed on Him, but they would not confess it". They did not want to be put out of the synagogue. They believed on Jesus.

It is possible to believe in Jesus and yet still be lost. We have indicated already that the devils believe in the Lord Jesus. Well, is it the moment we repent of our sins? Repentance is essential. Luke 13:3 "Jesus said, I tell you nay, except you who repent. You shall all likewise perish." We must repent of our wrongs. We must confess that Christ is the Son of God. (Matthew 10:32) Romans 10:10 "For with the heart man believeth unto righteousness and with the mouth confession is made unto salvation." But, there is an act that man does that changes his relationship from being outside of Christ to being inside of Christ. It is not when we believe. We do not believe into Christ. We do not repent into Christ. We do not confess into Jesus. The Bible says we are baptized into Christ. Galatians 3:26-27 "You are all the children of God by faith in Christ Jesus, for as many of you as have been baptized." How many Paul? As many of you, not one more or one less, as many of you that have been baptized into Christ have put on Christ. How do we get into Christ? We are baptized into Christ. That would be strange for me indeed to tell you how to come into this auditorium, ask you or command you, come into the auditorium because you are already here. In fact, you could not come into this auditorium unless you were outside of the auditorium. If you are in Christ at the time you believed you could not be baptized into Jesus Christ. Yet, the Bible says that as many of you that has been baptized into Christ have put on Christ. Romans 6 "What shall we say then? Shall we continue in sin that grace may abound? God forbid, how shall we that are dead to sin live any longer therein? No you are not, that so many of us that were baptized into Christ. We were baptized into his death. Therefore we are buried with him by baptism. Just like Christ was raised from the dead by the glory of the Father, even so we should walk in newness of life. If we have been planted together in the likeness of his death, we shall also be in the likeness of his resurrection." So, these scriptures indicate that we are baptized into Jesus Christ.

If you are here tonight and you have never obeyed the will of God. It is our hope and prayer that you will do so. Bible baptism involves baptism by the authority of Jesus. I baptized a man in Corbin, Kentucky who told me he was baptized because the preacher gave everybody a silver dollar that would be baptized. He was not baptized for the right reason. The religious word today teaches that you are to be baptized to show you have accepted Jesus as your savior, but you never read that terminology in God's word. We must be a proper subject for baptism. I have just been up in Iowa. Most of the people up there are baptized when they are little babies. I guess in that community, 80 percent of the people believe that when they were little babies they were baptized. But, the Bible says, "He that believeth and is baptized shall be saved." Then we must be baptized in water. See here is water, what hinders me from being baptized? You could be baptized in buttermilk and it would not be Bible baptism. Bible baptism is baptism in water and it is a burial. Romans 6:4 "We are buried with Him by baptism." Not sprinkled. Not having water poured on you, but we are buried with Him in baptism, for the remission of your sins. So, if you are saved before you are baptized, you were not baptized for the right reasons. The majority of the protestant world today teaches that you are saved before baptism and they do not baptize for the remission of sins. Our catholic friends baptize for the remission of sins. Only baptism known for hundreds of hundreds of even thousands of years until the protestant churches began to come into existence and say you are saved by faith as well as baptism is not essential. But, baptism is essential for it is for the remission of your sins.

If that be your desire tonight, we urge you to obey the will of God. If you are here and you have wandered away from God, we urge you to come back to Him. Will you come tonight as we stand together and sing?

THE POWER TO BECOME

When I (Dale) moved to work with the church at Granny White in Nashville Dad told me about one of the books that had most influenced his life. The book is the one he talks about in this sermon, "The Power to Become" by S.C. Boyce. One of the members at the church at Granny White was Juanita Boyce, S.C.'s, then, aging daughter. I asked her if she had anymore of that book and she had one extra copy and gave it to me. I wrapped it that year for Dad as a Christmas gift. He did love that book. We believe it is because Dad was a pure optimist. Perhaps his favorite two non-biblical quotes were: "The future is as bright as the promises of God" and "Attempt great things for God. Expect great help from God!" This shines through in this sermon presented on The Living Word.

J & D

Bro. S. O. Boyce, Sr. wrote a book a number of years ago titled Power To Become.

This book is now out of print but it has had a dramatic effect on the hearts and lives of many people. Dale Carnagie has written a book "How To Win Friends and Influence People" and there have been a number of other books written along the same idea that man has the ability to become whatever he wants to become. If I were giving this particular lesson a title, I would simply call it "The Power to Become." In John 1:11-12, the Apostle John says " He came unto His own and His own received Him not, but as many as received Him, He gave them power to become the sons of God, even to them that believe on His name." On tonights telecast, I want to discuss with you power to become a son of God.

What a great privilege it is that we as human beings have to become the sons of God. We far excel any other of God's creation in this particular area. He could have made us like the animals or like the trees, but the Bible says in Gen. 1:26-27 that man was made in the image of God. Man was given some of the eternal nature of God and so somewhere a thousand years from tonight, you will be in existence and I will be in existence. Man has a soul within him. The Bible says that the soul of man does not die in such passages as Ecclesiastes 12:7, "The body will return to the dust, but the spirit or soul will return to God that gave it." There are many great lessons that we can learn from these great passages that we have read.

In the first place, verse 11 talks about the fact that Jesus came to His own and His own did not receive Him. Many times, those that receive the greatest blessings are the least appreciative. Isn't that true, to some degree, of all of us. We receive blessings and we take these blessings for granted. Have you ever thought about the fact that the average monthly income of Russia if $100 and there are some countries in the Orient that if a man made over $100 a year, he would be above the average. My friends, even the very poorest of us in America far excel those of other parts of the world.

How blessed we are, but we are blessed in other ways. For example, we are blessed in that we have the Bible, the Word of God. Man can learn a great deal about God from nature because nature is a witness to the goodness and greatness of God. The Psalmist said, "The heavens declare the glory of God and the firmament showeth His handiwork." Yet without the Bible, we do not know about the love and concern and the nature of God.

We do not know about the wrath of God and the vengeance of God. In other words, we do not know the great characteristics of God but from the Bible. Those of us who have been born in this great country have access to the Bible. This is something many people do not have; many people do not enjoy. Many people do not have the opportunity to sit down and read the Bible. This is an opportunity that man in times passed have not enjoyed. There was a time when I understand that the Bibles were chained to the pulpits and it was against the law of certain churches that people did not have the right to read the Bible for themselves. We would cry out in protest but I really wonder tonight how many of us are students of the word of God. What a great privilege it is to be born in our country and to have many of the material and financial blessings, but also to have free access to the Word of God.

I would like to think with you for just a few moments that with every blessing and with every opportunity there also comes a responsibility. Think of a man that might die of thirst standing in a stream of bubbling water. We might say that something was wrong with him. Think about a man that lives next door to a grocery store, had access to a grocery store, but died of starvation. What a tragedy this would be. We would think that this man needed to be examined, that surely there must be something mentally wrong with him. But I raise the question to all of us tonight. You have access to the Word of God, could become His children, but simply refuse to do so. What a great privilege it is that any person viewing our television program tonight can become a child of God.

But there is another thought that we can gleen from this verse of scripture and it is that God gave to these people that we are going to mention in a few minutes, the right to become the sons of God. Salvation is a gift of God. Ephesians 2:8-9, "for by grace are ye saved, but not of yourselves, it is the gift of God, not of works lest any man should boast." So salvation is a gift of God. Titus 2:11-12 tells us that "the grace of God that bringeth salvation hath appeared to all men". Yet not all men are going to be saved. Jesus said there are more people that are going to be lost than there are that will be saved. Why? This must mean that the grace of God, though it is free and available to every person, will not be received by everyone. It is like the illustration that possibly I have used before on the television program. Six boys were outside of a ballgame. I go up to them and say, "Boys, would you like to go in to see the ballgame?" and they say, "Yes. Brother Jenkins, we would be delighted to go." I say, "Now boys, you understand that it won't cost you a thing, just go in." After awhile I go in and see 3 boys and say "weren't there 6 boys, where are the other 3?" They say that they chose not to go in. How did you get in? We got in by the goodness of Brother Jenkins or by the grace of Brother Jenkins in other words. The point is this gift was available to all, but all were not the recipients of it because not all choose to go in and see the ballgame. My friends, salvation is a gift available to us, but the question tonight is upon what terms does God want us to accept this gift. He says here, and we invite your careful consideration to John 1:11-12, "but He came unto his own and His own received Him not, but as many as received Him, to them He gave the power to become the sons of God, even to those that believe on His name. Notice especially the last phrase, that He gave some power to become His son that believed on his name. I would like to suggest to you that belief doesn't make one automatically a child of God. Yet you realize that many, many people in the Birmingham area think that if they believe on the Lord, that this in and of itself makes them a child of God. But you see, our faith or our belief gives us power, or as the margin says, gives us the right or gives us the privilege to become a son of God. Man is not saved by faith only, but this faith that we have gives us the right or privilege to become a son of God. I would like to illustrate it like this. Suppose that tonight I said to you that are fathers of sons that I am going to give your son the right to become your son. Well, that doesn't work, does it. I can't give your son the right to become your son, he is already your son. Now if I am a son of God at the time I believe, then John would be using incorrect phraseology to say that I am going to give those that believe the right to become sons of God.

In the New Testament, we have examples of believers who were lost. For example, we read in Acts 2 of some believers and these believers raised the question, "men and brethren, what should we do?" They believed in Christ, yet they were not saved because Peter tells them in verse 38 "repent and be baptized everyone of you in the name of Jesus Christ for the remission of your sins and ye shall receive the give of the Holy Ghost." In Acts 8, we read of some Samaritans who believed, yet they were not saved by this faith only. They needed also to repent of their sins and they were baptized. So faith in and of itself does not automatically make us a child of God but it gives us the right to become a Christian.

What kind of faith do you have? There are two kinds of faith, there is an active faith and an inactive faith. There is a strong faith and a weak faith. There is a living, dynamic faith, but there is also a weak and frail faith. What kind of faith do you have?

The kind of faith that saves is an obedient faith. So I would like to suggest to you tonight that if you believe in the Lord, you have the right to become His son and you can become His son by repenting of your sins, Luke 13:B, by confessing His name, Rom. 10:10, and by being baptized for the remission of your sins Mark 16:16. What a grand privilege it is tonight that we have to become the sons of God.

WHY DID JESUS DIE?

It is indeed a great honor for me to have the opportunity to stand in this pulpit again and I thank all of you. I know there are many things that you could be doing at this hour and many places you could be but you have chosen to come together to study the word of God. This is indeed encouraging. Thank you so much for that decision you have made. I have enjoyed immensely the meeting. Enjoyed so much the wonderful meal we had again this evening. I understand you have 4 songs here so it looks like we may have to extend the meeting another night to take care of all of the songs. I don't know how that is going to work out but we are scheduled to close the meeting tomorrow night and I hope you will be present for that service as we talk a little bit concerning the future and I hope that you will make your plans. If you have to miss any service, please don't let it be tomorrow night and just make your plans to come and to be present.

We are to be students of the word of God. The apostle Paul said to the preacher Timothy, preach the word. He said I charge thee before God and the Lord Jesus Christ who shall judge the quick and the dead in His appearing and in His Kingdom. Preach the word. Be instant, in season, out of season, reprove, rebuke, exhort with all long suffering in doctrine. He said the day is coming when men shall not want to listen to sound preaching but they will turn unto themselves teachers having itching ears. He said they will be turned to fables. I believe to some extent that could be said about any generation but certainly we would be applicable in the world in which we live in today. The last book of the Bible, the book of Revelation chapter 20 verse 12, the Bible says I saw the dead small and great stand before God and the books were open and another book was open which is the book of life and the dead were judged out of the books according to their works. So we are going to be judged in light of what the word of God says, therefore it behooves all of us to do the Will of God. I am sure you are here tonight because you want to go to heaven and because you appreciate the great sacrifice that God has made. I believe there are 3 motivations for us to serve God.

Motivation #1 would be the motivation of fear. Fear is a legitimate motivation. We ought to scare people in to serving God. Jesus did, for example the word translated hell is the word Gehenna. It is found 12 times in scripture, 11 times it is employed by our Lord Jesus Christ himself. Our Lord told about the rich man and Lazarus. The rich man died and four times the state of that rich man is described as being a place of torment. Our Lord would tell us it is a fearful thing to be lost and yet if you are motivated only by fear you will do the minimum. How often do I have to come to services? How much do I have to give? If that is your only motivation then you will do the very minimum that you can do in service to God.

There is another motivation and that is what is in it for me. That is a ligament question. Peter asked that question one time and the Lord did not rebuke him and say oh Peter you ought to be ashamed of yourself. Your motive is not correct in serving me but our Lord answered his question. There is motivation for us to go to heaven because of what is in it for us. Motivation to serve God that God will hear and answer our prayers. Then God will give us peace that passes understanding. God will give us insight into the purposes of life that we have.

Then of course, there is the great blessing of heaven itself where we will be able to be with God forever and forevermore. There is a third motivation and that is the one that we are trying to talk about tonight. That is the motivation of great appreciation. Being thankful and grateful for all that God has done for us. The person that serves God, will out of an overflow of appreciation for the blessings that he has, is the one that will go the second mile. He will be the one that will do everything within his power to be an effective servant of God. So tonight, I want to talk with you concerning that motivation of going to heaven and out of appreciation for all that the Lord has done for us.

The word cross is an interesting word. The form of the word or lack of the word is a word crux and we sometimes talk about the fact that this is the crux of the matter. That is central to the matter. It is a very center piece of the matter. The cross is the very center of Christianity. As the sun, planets, stars revolve around the planets, and revolve around the sun and so Christianity revolves around the cross of Jesus Christ. No wonder the apostle Paul would say in 1 Corinthians chapter 2:2, I determined not to know anything among you, save Jesus Christ, and Him crucified. That is about the cross of Jesus and Paul said I want to preach about Jesus and about the crucifixion of Jesus and I determined not to know other things but I want you to understand that the very crux of the matter in Christianity is the cross. I determined not to preach anything other than the cross. Now Paul was well qualified. Paul no doubt was familiar with Greek mythology. No doubt Paul knew Roman philosophy. There is no doubt that Paul was highly familiar with the law of Moses. He was trained at the feet of

Gamaliel, the great learned scholar of the ancient world. He was
a man who knew all of these things and yet Paul said, "I
determine not to know anything among you except Jesus Christ
and Him crucified." I am fearful brethren sometimes that I
listen to the story of the cross so frequently that may be I do not
appreciate the cross like I really should. There is a possibility
that we become so familiar with the cross of Jesus that it loses it
impact upon our lives and may it never be so but that is a real
and genuine possibility. Our Lord lived a forsaken life. Our
Lord's brothers did not believe in him, his half brothers, until
after the resurrection. After the resurrection, they became
devout followers of his. Before the resurrection of Jesus, John
chapter 7 says they did not believe in Jesus. They did not accept
the fact that He was the Son of God. I do not know how many
miracles they may have seen him perform. I do not know how
many sermons they may have heard him preach but they did not
accept Jesus. He was forsaken by his own family. He was
forsaken by his own community. The town of Nazareth turned
on him. I have been to the city of Nazareth in Israel. I have seen
that great mountain cliff where evidently they were going to
throw Jesus over that cliff but Jesus escaped from their presence.
He was rejected by his own town. He was rejected even by God
himself. He cried out on the cross, the fourth statement that he
made, My God, my God why has thou forsaken me. Our Lord
lived an abandoned life. When he was a young man of only 33
years of age, they took him out and the scourged him. They beat
him unmercifully. Many times those that were being scourged
would cry out for their beaters to take their own life because
they could bear the pain no more. I don't know whether you
have been in very much pain or not but our Lord knew the
intensity of pain. He knew what it was like to be hurting. He

knew what it was like to be at the point of death because of the hurt that he had. Then of course, they took him out the lonely way, Via Dolorosa way and there they executed him upon the cross and for 6 agonizing hours our Lord slowly bled to death and He died because He loves you and because He loves me. May our little flimsy excuses never be paramount in our mind and may we with all the fervor of our being serve God daily in our lives and hourly in our lives may our life be committed o Him. Well that was a 10 minute introduction. I apologize for going a little long but I wanted us to think about the death of Jesus.

The question is why did Jesus die. I want to give some reasons why Jesus died. Reason #1, our Lord Jesus Christ died according to the teaching of God's word to take away the old law of Moses. In Colossians chapter 2:14, "Blotting out the handwriting of ordinances that was against us, which was contrary to us, and took it out of the way nailing it to his cross; the cross made possible the taking away of the old law of Moses." Our Lord died in order that the old law might be eradicated in order that we might serve God. I am so grateful tonight that I do not live under the law of Moses. Man who lived under the law of Moses could have many wives. David had 7 wives that we know by name. Solomon had 700 wives. Little boy said 300 porcupines but 300 concubines. One thousand woman, I can't even begin to imagine. This great wealthy man, the wealthiest King Israel would ever have. He died in order there might be the love between a husband and wife and that love might be as deep as it could possibly be. I am grateful Jesus died in order that old law might be taken away. I am thankful we do not have to confess our sins to a priest. Under that old law you would acknowledge your wrong and the priest would tell you the sacrifice and often even make that sacrifice for you in order that the sin might be forgiven. It was actually as you know not forgiven until the cross but they understood that they would be by faith would be forgiven of their sins just as we look back to the cross, we look forward to the time because of the sweet promises God had made. I am grateful tonight that I do not have to confess my sins to a man and that I confess my sins to God. Yet, there are hundreds and thousands of people tonight who go confess their sins to a man and expect that man to tell them how they can be forgiven. It is up to his discretion as to how or what role they will have to play in order to be forgiven. I am grateful tonight that we do not live under the old law because we would worship on Saturday and their would be the Sabbath day regulations. You couldn't even walk a mile. I have been there in Jerusalem from the Mt. Olives where our Lord ascended back to the wall city of Jerusalem was about 1 mile and it is indeed less than a mile. I have been there and been along that way. You could not even go further than that. One man who was a Sabbatarian was picked up and was hitch hiking back in the days when it was a little bit safer than it is today to pick up somebody that needed a ride and in the course of conversation found out the man was a member of the church that believed in worship on the Sabbath day and it was Saturday. We had traveled about 15 miles and I called that to his attention and he said well the walking is equivalent to 20 miles riding in an automobile. I do not know how he arrived at that. I have some very dear friends that are Rabbi's. We have 3 Jewish groups there in the city of Birmingham. The old Orthodox is the one I know best and it is interesting to me to talk with him and listen to his concepts about the Sabbath days and its regulations. He told me for example that you could not turn on a light on the Sabbath day from sundown Friday until sundown Saturday. If the light is on you may leave it on but you cannot turn a light on. You cannot travel in an automobile. The synagogue, there where they have been for sometime, they are moving the synagogue about 20 miles away from its present location. Guess what, all the members of that synagogue are having to move with it because they can't travel more than a mile on the day of worship. Interesting indeed. No television at all. Children could not go to a ball game on Friday nights. They live this way and we say how shameful it is that they have to abide by all of these rules and regulations. The Rabbi said you know we have never had a teenager arrested who was a member of the orthodox in the city of Birmingham. Isn't that amazing. I am glad I don't live under that old law though even though some of the regulations might help us to be more moral people than sometimes we are. I am grateful I don't live under that old law. That law was blotted out. Look at the 3 phrases. Blotted out, taken away, and nailed to the cross. In Matthew chapter 5 the Bible says that Jesus came in to the world and His purpose for coming according to this verse, he said, Think not that I am come to destroy the law, or the prophets I am not come to destroy but to fulfill. Lord why did you come, I came to fulfill. Lord were you successful in what you came to do. He said I came to fulfill the law, verily I say unto you. Till heaven and earth pass, one jot or one tittle shall in no wise pass from the law, till all be fulfilled. Question: was Jesus able to do what he came to do? He came to fulfill the law. I believe he was and that law was to last until it was fulfilled. One crossing of the t and dotting of the I would not pass until it was all fulfilled and our Lord was able to accomplish this. It was fulfilled and according to Paul's statement it was done away with at the cross of Jesus Christ.

Jesus did not lie beloved and Jesus was able to fulfill his purpose, therefore, I am grateful that Jesus died upon the cross because he did away with the old law of Moses. In the second place, Jesus died in order that the new covenant might be ratified with his blood. Blood was the sign of ratification of old covenants. You remember in the book of Genesis, God told Abraham to take some animals in chapter 15 beginning along verse 8, and he said take a heifer that is 3 years of age and a she-goat that is 3 years of age, and a ram that is 3 years of age. There Abraham did and he cut these animals in 2 and he stood there in the presence of them and God made a covenant with Abraham that through thy seed will all nations of the earth be blessed. I will make thee populous and your descendants will be as the sands of the seashore and as the stars of the heaven. God made a covenant and that covenant was ratified by the blood of these animals. The cross of Jesus indicates to us that we no longer have to keep those old laws that were given in the days of Abraham. The old law of Moses was ratified by the blood of Jesus. In Hebrews chapter 9, Moses called the people together and he spoke to them the Bible says the law and he took the blood of a calf and the blood of a goat and he sprinkled both the book and the people. That law was ratified by the blood of the covenant of these animals and that was a sign that this law was effective. With that background, Jesus said in Matthew 26 and 28, on the night before he was to be executed the next morning at 9:00 a.m., as he took the fruit of the vine he said this is my blood which is shed for the remission of sins. So Jesus shed his blood for the remission of our sins. We are redeemed because of that sacrifice that was made and the blood that was offered over 2,000 years ago. The covenant was ratified by the blood of Jesus Christ and I am so grateful for that. Before Jesus died upon the cross, our Lord could forgive mens sins for any reason that he saw fit. Just like when you make out a will, before you make that will out you may dispense your income, blessings, or possessions anyway you see fit but after your death that covenant takes over. So Jesus could dispense his blessings. One time there was a man who was paralyzed. He had 4 dear friends that picked him up on some kind of a mat. They took him to Jesus but because of the throng of people they could not get near Jesus. So they did the ingenious thing, they let the man down through the roof of the building and Jesus seeing their faith said to this man, thy sins be forgiven thee. Arise, and this man arose, and took up his pallet and left there on his own two feet and had never walked a day in his life. Now he was able to go about. We read also in the book of Luke chapter 7, Jesus was at the home of a man by the name of Simon and he was a Pharisee. There was a lady there that came and she began to bathe Jesus' feet with her tears and dry his feet with her hair. Jesus said to this woman, thy sins be forgiven thee. As long as Jesus wanted to, he could forgive men's sins for any reason that he wanted to forgive men's sins. The thief on the cross, Luke chapter 23, Jesus said to the thief, today thy shall be with me in paradise. He did not say you have to repent of your sins. He did not say you had to acknowledge your faith. He did not say you have to be baptized. The thief may have formally been baptized because John the Baptist baptized folks all around the Judea region. He could have been baptized, I don't know. There is a possibility he might have been baptized but it really doesn't matter because Jesus said today thy shalt be with me in paradise. The man was saved but he was saved prior to the death of Jesus. After the death of Jesus the will of Jesus became effective. Jesus said in Mark 16:16, He that believeth and is baptized shall be saved but he that believeth not shall be damned. In the day of Pentecost, these people responsible for the execution of Jesus, at least they had voted that Jesus die upon the cross, and they said to Peter, the rest of the apostles, men and brethren what shall we do. Peter said, repent and be baptized every one of you in the name of Jesus Christ for the remission of sins and ye shall receive the gift of the Holy Ghost. So baptism is one of the requirements that God has for our redemption. Forgiveness takes place not a long time before we are baptized.

Sometimes there are those say that they were saved and much later there was baptism. You know the Bible only taught that one time would be enough but the Bible never teaches that. Every passage that mentions baptism and salvation together, baptism always precedes. There is not a single exception to that. Jesus said he that believeth and is baptized. Where is salvation, it is after baptism. On the day of Pentecost, repent and be baptized every one of you in the name of Jesus Christ for the remission of your sins. Where is remission of sins? It is after baptism and not before baptism. Acts 22:16, Ananias a certain disciple came to Saul of Tarus and said, and now why tarriest now?, arise and be baptized and wash away thy sins calling on the name of the Lord. Our sins are washed away by the blood of Jesus but we are baptized in to the death of Jesus. We receive the benefit of his shed blood at the time we are baptized. How grateful we are that the truth is so plain and so clear. Jesus died in order that the law, his new covenant, would be ratified and it was ratified in his blood. Thirdly, Jesus died in order to make possible the church. In Acts 20:28, Paul said to the elders of Ephesus on the island of Miletus, take heed therefore unto yourselves, and to all the flock, over the which the Holy Ghost hath made you overseers, to feed the church of God, which he hath purchased with his own blood. He purchased the church with his blood.

Ephesians 5:25, "Husbands love your wives even as Christ also loved the church and gave himself for it." Jesus died for the church. Jesus gave himself for it. 1 Corinthians 6:19-20, "You are not your own you are bought with a price therefore glorify God with your body and in your spirit which are His." What was the price that was paid for our redemption? It was the cross of Jesus Christ. You know we give our life for things that are important to us. A man will die for his country. I talked to a young man today who left at 6 o'clock this evening if all went according to schedule, on his way over to Iraq. He said to me, Brother Jerry, I hope I get back but if I don't please tell my wife I love her and care for her. A man will die, give his life, for his country. A man will give his life for his family. Sometimes there have been those who had to risk their own life. Don't tell me that our Lord was so naive that he gave his life for something that is not even essential and that it is optional as to whether the church is important in your life. Jesus said upon this rock I will build my church and the gates of hell shall not prevail against it. So I am suggesting to you tonight that Jesus died in order that the church might be established. The church should be important in our lives. In Matthew chapter 16:18, Jesus said I will build my church and he gave his life as we indicated for the establishment of the church. Matthew 6:33, seek ye first the kingdom of God and his righteousness and all of these things shall be added unto you. Several years ago there were some boys that were playing on a ball team. They were pretty good and they got to play for the championship for the city up in Huntsville, Alabama. They put the championship game, guess what, on Wednesday night. Well one of the boys, who happened to be my father, was not as good as the other 3 guys but he said I am going to go to services on Wednesday night. The coach, after the other 3 ball players, ,4 of them in all on the team that went to the West Huntsville Church of Christ, said we can't show up. We have to go to services. The coach went to the officials and they had the game delayed for them an hour so these boys would have time to go to services. Well, my grandfather and my Uncle Willy got in an argument that night. I don't know what they were arguing about, probably was the difference in mercy and grace or some theological question like that. Anyway, they got in a big argument and class went on, and on, and on, extended further and further. Folks at the ballpark got to asking what are we waiting on, why isn't the game starting on time? Somebody let them know it was because 3 boys were at the church of Christ and they were in a Bible study at the church. All that night when they get up they would call them preacher and that kind of thing but there were thousands of people that night that respected that decision of these young men. Yet today, it is not uncommon for parents to take their children out of services on Sunday night or say you have too much homework you don't need to go to services tonight or Wednesday night. The Bible says the Lord's kingdom purchased by the blood of Jesus is to be first in our life. Seek ye first the kingdom of God. Not second or third. Seek ye first. I have known members of the church go on vacation, may be not even worship God and if they couldn't line up their dates exactly right they would miss the service Sunday morning, come back and take the Lord's supper on Sunday night. I have often wondered how they would feel if the Lord came that Sunday morning while they were traveling back home from a vacation they had taken. Beloved, we just need to seek the kingdom of God first in our life. This is what the Bible says. Jesus died in order that the church might be established. Finally, I would suggest to you tonight that Jesus died to demonstrate the depth of his love for all of us. Our Lord loved us and the Bible says in John 15:13, "Greater love hath no man shown than this, that a man lay down his life for his friends." Yet what the Bible says is while we were enemies, while we were wayward, and while we were not walking and living as God wanted us to live Christ died for the ungodly. Romans 5:8, "God commendeth his love toward us, in that, while we were yet sinners, Christ died for us." Why did Jesus die? Well he wanted you to know how much he loved you. He could have taken the clouds and written across the clouds I love you. He could have chiseled out with his finger in granite on a mountaintop somewhere, I love you but our Lord did not choose to do that. Our Lord wanted you. Our God wanted us to all know the extent of the love he had for us. Beloved if you were the only person upon the face of the earth, Jesus still would have died for you. Hebrews 2:9, But we see Jesus, who was made a little lower than the angels for the suffering of death, crowned with glory and honor; that he by the grace of God should taste death for every man. He died for you, I don't care who you are, how much you have or do not have, how educated or uneducated you may be, he died for you. God wanted you to know how much I love you. Somebody said he said I love you this much and he died upon the cross at Calvary. Many years ago, I heard about a young man that committed a crime. He was sentenced to many, many years in jail. His wife did everything she could to get him out of jail. She would work hours unbelievable, almost all day and all night ruining her health trying to get up enough money so she could hire a lawyer to get him out of prison. She was successful. When he got out of prison after about a few weeks, he saw another lady that he was more interested in and he left his wife. I don't know how you feel about somebody like that but I think a fellow like that ought to be taken out and horsewhipped. Think of sometimes of how we do our Lord. Our Lord died in order that you may know how much he loved you. The rest of our lives we need to serve him in the most effective way that we possibly can. We must live for him. We must teach our children, our grandchildren. We must teach our friends and our neighbors to live for him.

Tonight if you are not a New Testament Christian, Jesus died for you and it is our hope that tonight you will obey the gospel if you believe with all your heart in Jesus, willing to repent of your sins, confess the name of Christ in I believe Jesus is the Son of God, and be immersed in the waters of baptism for the remission of your sins, you can be saved. If I said tonight if you will believe and be baptized I will give you $500,000. I think all of us could understand, and probably all of us, would come gladly to receive the $500,000. Salvation is worth far more than $500,000. Jesus said he that believeth and is baptized shall be saved. There is no reason tonight why anybody should leave this auditorium lost in sin. If you are here and have not been faithful to God, regular in your attendance, living, talking or acting like a Christian should and you need to be restored to your first love we invite you to come as together we stand and sing.

THE TWENTY TRUTHS ABOUT WORRY

Worry –
   we all do it!!
we all struggle w/ it.

Philp 4:6
Matt 6:33

About my children. I will be able to control so nothing bad will happen to them. If I worry about my husband, my marriage, my job, or economy that if someway if I worry about these things that which is uncontrollable will be controlled by my worry. That is a myth and it will only bring us misery. There are commands in the Bible that are more difficult than other commands to obey. It is not hard to obey the commandment thy shall not kill. I suppose most of us have obeyed that commandment pretty regularly in this assembly. Thou shall not steal, thou shall not commit adultery but there is a command of the Bible that is really a difficult command for us to obey. It is found in the book of Philippians 4:6 and it says, don't worry about anything. What is that Paul? Don't worry about anything. Now you talk about a difficult command, that is a hard command. The word worry, the English word worry, means to strangle or to choke and that is what worry does. Worry strangles out our lives and chokes away our happiness. The Greek word for worry is a word which means divided. All of you that suffer from anxieties and those of you who are depressed, you know that something that will really create depression and anxiety will be when you have a divided mind, when there is internally a tug of war pulling at you and it only makes you miserable. Well aren't you glad that the book that gives the answers to all of life problems also deals with the problem of worry. This marvelous book that God has given to us gives a solution for worry. This morning I want to begin the lesson as there are only 2 major points in my lesson but I want to begin the lesson by talking with you about 5 things that Jesus tells us the truth about worry. If you have your outline we will go slowly so you can fill those outlines in.

1) Jesus said that worry is unreasonable. If you have your Bible please look to Matthew chapter 6:25. Therefore I say unto you, take no fault for your life, what you shall eat or what you shall drink nor yet for your body what you shall put on. Is not life more than meat and the body that raiment? Now we tend to worry but why do we worry and why is worry unreasonable. Number one it is unreasonable because we worry about things that are unnecessary to worry about. We worry in fact about the wrong things. We worry about instead of being concerned about our soul and about our relationship with God and about avoiding hell and going to heaven, we worry about things like go to a party and getting something spilled on our dress or on our coat, tie or shirt. I have seen some folks almost have a coronary because of a shirt. If you go down to Walmart where I get my shirts it wouldn't be such a big problem but many people really are concerned about the things that are exterior rather than the things that are eternal. In addition, we worry about things we cannot change and that is useless to worry about these things. If you can change things don't worry about it, get busy and make those changes. If you can't change how useless it is to worry about these things.

Secondly, worry is illogical. It is irrational. It is unreasonable because it exaggerates the problem. Somebody says something to you of a critical nature, maybe its job, maybe its school and they say something to you and you begin to be concerned about that. Are you listening young folks. That keeps on growing over, over, and over in your life. It just keeps on building up and it becomes really bigger than it is. Worry therefore, is unreasonable. Not only that, worry is unnatural. Look at verse 26, behold the fowls of the air for they sow not neither do they reap nor gather in the barns yet your heavenly father feedeth them, are ye not much better than they. Down in verse 28, why take thee thought for raiment, consider the lilies of the field, how they grow, they toil not, neither do they spin. Now Jesus gives us a lesson from nature. I am not an ornithologist. We have a lady in this church that watches birds. Her name is Marie Earwood and she was my partner a couple of years ago and may be even other times we got to knock on doors together there in Central America and we would be walking along and all of the sudden, she is like look at that, look at that and maybe a quarter of a mile away she will see some little ole bird and she will begin to give its historical background, knows it name, knows it scientific name. I don't know much about birds. Seems to me that kind of birds are useless creatures. I mean they build a nest once a year, they float around, they pick up land that could be developed, they twitter, they sing. They are pretty but really they don't do a lot but you know God takes care of the birds. You talk about a welfare system, birds are on God's welfare system. The Bible says I take care of birds and you are better than a bird and I am going to take care of you. Then Jesus moves from bird watching to a lesson from botany. He says look at the flowers, look at the intricacy of flowers. Look at the beauty of those little flowers and some of them are only going to last a few weeks and some of them last only 6 months but they are not going to be around very long yet God has taken such detail and such time to make them a work of art. Here is the point. God looks after the animals. God looks after the flowers. You are better than an animal and a flower but let me tell you something, animals don't worry and plants don't worry. The only thing in all of creation that I know of that worries is man. Psalms 145:16 says that God satisfies the desire of every living thing and the animals understand this verse. Psalms 145:16, but someway or another we have not understood this particular verse. Worry is not only unreasonable it is unnatural for people to worry. You might say well brother Jerry I am a born worrier. I worry all the time but let me suggest to you that you learned this. You learned it from your parents, your peers, partners, and other people. You see worry is something that is a learned response and the good news is that if worry can be learned it can also be unlearned. You don't have to be a worry wart for the rest of your life. Some of you have been practicing and you have gotten real good at it. You have done it so much and it takes it out on our bodies. We get all kind of headaches and ulcers. Have you ever heard anybody say man I am worried sick, well there is some proof in that. Worry can make you sick. When you are in the outline write down 2 verses I believe I left these off, Proverbs 12:25, heaven is in the heart of man maketh it stoop. We would say that worry weights a man down and it does. Then in Proverbs 14:40, a heart at peace gives hope to the body. You know worry is fatiguing. It makes us more tired than hard work. Have you ever sit up at the hospital, may be sit up all night long at the hospital and you feel so tired, more tired than if you had gone out and worked for 10 hours digging a ditch. Why is that? Because worry makes us fatigued and your Father knows your needs. He didn't say the father of the birds know your needs or the father of the flowers, he said Your Father knows your needs, that is what he is saying.

In the third place, worry is unhelpful. Jesus said it doesn't work. Look at verse 27, which of you by taking thought can add one cubit to his stature? The NIV says which of you by worrying can add a single hour to his life. Worry will not, not make you taller, it will not make you shorter, it will not make you thinner, worry doesn't work. It is like sitting in a rocking chair. There is a lot of motion to it but you don't go very far it has not progress. The book of Philippians says in chapter 4:19, we are not to worry and when you worry about the past it does not change the past. When you worry about the future it does not give you control of the future. Worry only messes up today. So worry is not helpful.

In the fourth place, worry is unnecessary. Now this is the real meat of what Jesus is saying here in Matthew chapter 6. He says wherefore is God so clothed the grass of the field which today is and tomorrow is cast in to the oven. Shall he not much more cloth you oh ye of little faith. There is no need to worry because he says that God will take care of you. He is your heavenly father. How many of you get an allowance or got an allowance, can I see your hand? Oh yeah, several of you get an allowance. You know when I was growing up and we got a little allowance, I never did think about where my Dad got that money. I didn't know until I was in college that we were poor. I always thought we had everything we needed, which we actually did. We did not have as much as some other folks did and I never one time ever remembered wondering about where did my Dad get the money to send us to Athens Bible School. I never one time worried about things like that. Why is it therefore that when it comes to God we get all perturbed about that. God says you don't have to worry about your next paycheck. He says I will take care of you, I will supply your needs. That is what the verse says in Philippians 4:19 that my

God shall supply all of your need. Does that include the car payment. Does that include the mortgage payment, the doctor bill? Does that include the shoes. Would you agree there is a difference, however, in greed and need. It doesn't say God will supply all of my greed. It does say that God will take care of my needs. Worry always indicates that we have a misunderstanding of the nature of God. If I don't understand what God is like, I will not trust him. If I do not trust God then I will worry. The real issue is who you believe God is. Well you say God is the one that makes salvation possible. Well isn't it strange that we trust God for salvation. We can believe that God can deliver us from sin and that Jesus has prepared a place for the redeemed. We know that God can save us from how bad we have been and how wicked and evil we have been, we can understand that principal but that God cannot take care of our needs. How ludicrous is this? We are like a man that was hiking along with a nap sack on his back and a pick up truck comes by and the man offers him a ride. He gets in the truck and the man says why don't you throw your knapsack back in the back of the truck. He says now listen buddy if you will just take care of me I will take care of the knapsack. So we say to God if you take care of my salvation, I will take care of all of these other matters.

Jesus in the fifth place says worry is unchristian. You know when you worry you act like an atheist? You act like a heathen, an infidel when you worry. He said while the atheist and pagans seek after these things. They don't have the assurance that you have. You act like God does not exist. Now if you are an unbeliever in this assembly today, I will say to you, brother you need to worry. You need to pick up the newspaper and see all the killings going on and all the illness and you need to worry.

An unbeliever needs to worry. An atheist, infidel, agnostic, you need to worry but a Christian why indeed not because we have a heavenly father.

In a few moments, please do not pick up the song books yet, I am not closing but I want to suggest to you what the Bible says we must do in becoming a Christian. Number one we must believe in Jesus and trust in the Lord with all of our hearts that he indeed is the son of God. Do you believe that? Then why don't you act like it. If you really do believe in Jesus Christ and that he is the son of God, what difference has he made in your life. Have you repented of your sins? Have you stood before an assembly and made that noble confession that I believe Jesus to be the son of God. Have you been buried with your Lord in the watery tomb of baptism. Jesus said he that believeth and is baptized shall be saved. Have you been raised a new creature with a new name with new goals and aspirations? Tuesday night there was a young man who had earlier written me a 2 page letter. He was in a real bind. His wife had left him taking with her 2 children and had run off with another man. She had gotten him fired from his job by constant calling and lying about him. She had charged every credit card they had to the max. Deprived him of privileges of seeing his children. He said what can I do? I didn't know anything to tell him but to give his life to Christ. I mean this fellow was in such a mess. I don't know what kind of situation you are in but I am saying to you today that if you are not a Christian that you have a lot to worry about but if you are a child of God in this dog eat dog world in Birmingham, Alabama you do not need to worry because God says I will take care of you. Don't act like a non-cared for orphan. The Bible says that God knows every need

that you have. One of these days we will learn we cannot
control that God is in control. If you worry you are acting like
an atheist or an unwanted orphan. Besides that it is a very poor
way to be a good Christian to encourage others to become
children of God. The message that you give is not a very
powerful message. If you are going around telling the people
where you work about all of the problems you have and acting
like you don't have a heavenly father. Going around in school
acting as though you are an unwanted orphan as far as God's
family is concerned. I want to give the antidote to worry before
we quit this morning and I have 4 ½ minutes. Before we go to
the second part of our lesson, however, I want to stop right
here. I would like for you to write in the outline the greatest
worry you have. Would you just jot down on that little outline.
This is the greatest worry that I have and if it is the person
sitting next to you just draw an arrow. I mean God will know
who you are talking about. Now scribble it out, just draw a line
through it. Now would you write down the next biggest thing
you worry about. Do you have something in mind? I believe you
do, you look real worried. Now I want to give you what Jesus
said of how to get rid of worry. Not only does Jesus give us 5
reasons why we should not worry, he says there are 3 steps that
all of us can take that will help us to get rid of any worry that
we have.

1) We need to put God first in every area of our life.
Matthew 6:32, for the pagans run after these things. Your
heavenly father knows that you need them but seek ye first the
kingdom of God and his righteousness and all of these things
shall be added unto you. Worry is a warning light. It says you
have your values all mixed up and whenever I start worrying it

means that something is out of whack in my life. Something is taking the place of God in my life and that God is not number one in my life. It may be in a dating relationship. It may be in recreation or jobs. Whenever God is not number 1 in my life there is an area of worry. Let God be number one. Take my life oh Father, mold it. Take my life and let it be. Do we really mean those statements. Now every person has decided who or what they are going to live for. You tell me the answer, who are you living for and what are you living for, I will tell you whether you worry or not. If you are living for something than to glorify and honor Him than you are going to be plagued for the rest of your life. Some of you may be living for money. People have gotten more than they can spend in their lifetime and sit around worrying about money all of the time. They worry about losing it. They worry about saving it, investing it, protecting it, and about maintaining it. All we need to do is put God first. I am asking you this morning, is God number one in every area of your life.

2) Live one day at a time. This is the second thing that Jesus said about worry. He said in verse 34: take therefore no thought for tomorrow for tomorrow shall take thought from the things of itself sufficient under the day is the evil thereof. Don't open up your umbrella until it starts raining. Some of you say it is going so good in life I know something bad is going to happen. Things are just going too smoothly. In my relationship with my companion, things are going so beautifully, I know something bad is about to happen. Don't open up the umbrella until it starts to rain. There are 2 days in the week that you should never worry about. You should never worry about yesterday and you should never worry about today. Today is tomorrow is the

tomorrow you worried about yesterday. Now it is alright to plan for tomorrow. I am not saying that we shouldn't plan. God wants us to plan but I am saying we need to depend upon God one day at a time. Isn't it interesting that when Jesus taught his disciples to pray. He said after this manner you are to pray, give us our yearly food, no, give us our monthly food, no give us our daily bread. One day at a time. He wants us to depend upon him moment by moment.

3) Trust God to care for the things that are beyond your control. In verse 30, he says, oh ye of little faith. Now worry and trust just don't live together. When worry comes in to the heart, faith goes out the back door because they simply will not live together. Paul said be careful for nothing but in everything by prayer and supplication with thanksgiving let your request be made known unto God and listen to this glorious promise, and the peace of God which passeth all understanding shall keep your hearts and minds through Jesus Christ. We either panic or we pray. If there is anything that is not worth praying about it is not worth worrying about. In Romans 8:32, Paul said, God did not spare his own son but God gave him up for all of you. How will he not also along with him graciously give us all things. How much does God love you? He loves you enough that he gave his own son. Paul said based upon this, God will give unto us all things that we need.

In closing today, I remind you of the story of Jehoshaphat. It is found in 2 Chronicles chapter 20. There were those that came to Jehoshaphat and said there cometh a great multitude against thee beyond the sea on this side of Syria. In verse 10, behold the children of Ammon, Moab and mount Seir whom thy wouldest not let Israel invade , when they came out of the land Egypt, but they turned from them, and destroyed them not. He says they are coming after you. Three magnificent armies with weaponry and determination to wipe Israel off the face of the earth and the prophet said to Jehoshaphat, harken ye ole Judah and you inhabitants of Jerusalem and thou King Jehoshaphat thus saith the Lord unto you be not afraid, be not dismayed by reason of this great multitude for the battle is not yours it is God's. If you need God will you come as together we stand and sing.

Dad preached on giving every Sunday the month of November for years.

Dad believed what one gave was a best measure of spiritual growth. The average giving per week went up every year for 44 years but one— 1972. In the midst of the oil crisis and some challenges brought on by a congregational riff over the busing program they did not increase the budget and did not increase in their giving.

Dad believed the congregation needed a challenge that forced people to consider their giving. He believed that if Christians knew better they would do better. He also believed that part of the mission of leaders was to put a challenge in front of the church to give them something to reach for.

J & D

In a circle that the missionary had drawn. The missionary said I am afraid that is not sufficient. Then the old Indian took his squaw, his wife and children, and placed them in the circle and he said to the missionary I am willing to give these, my loved ones, to the Lord. Again the missionary said I am afraid that won't do either. Finally the old Indian said I have nothing left and he stepped inside the circle.

In Rom. 12:1, Paul said, "I beseech you, therefore, brethren by the mercies of God, that ye present your bodies a living sacrifices, holy acceptable unto God, which is your reasonable service." On this morning's telecast, I want to continue our study of worship with you. In John 4:24, Jesus said, "God is a spirit; and they that worship him must worship him in spirit and in truth."

There are four kinds of worship described in the New Testament. In Colossians 1, there is what is called will worship. That is, a man worships God according to his own will. In Matt. 15:9, Jesus said, "But in vain do they worship me, teaching for doctrines the commandments of men." In Acts 17:30-33, the Apostle Paul talks about ignorant worship. Here is this passage we have a description of true worship.

There are three requirements of true or acceptable worship. First, we must worship the right object; namely, we must worship God. Secondly, we must worship God in spirit. Among other things, this means that our attitude must be right. Third, we must worship God in truth. John 17:17 says, "Sanctify them through thy truth, thy word is truth."

How do we worship God in truth? By worshipping Him according to the way that His word tells us to worship. We can't worship God in just any way. If a man has the ability to lift 100-200 lbs and he says that he does this to the glory of God or if a woman has the ability to bake the finest chocolate pie you have ever seen and she says she does this to the glory of God, that does not mean that she is paying homage or paying respect in praising God in the way that God wants to be praised. We must worship God in truth and this we can only ascertain by a study of the word of God.

We have studied with you already that we are to worship God by the breaking of bread or the observance of the Lord's Supper. We are to worship God also, as we noted last week, through praying to God. Today we want to study with you the subject of giving.

I know that giving is not a very popular thing and there are no doubt those who view our telecast will say there goes another preacher talking about the subject of giving. Are you aware of the fact that there is a great deal said in the Bible about the subject of giving. For example, one out of every six verses, it has been as certained, in the Gospels deals with the subject of giving. Of the 38 parables that our Lord taught, 18 deal with the subject of giving. Our Lord talked a great deal about giving.

It is not that we want to fatten our own pocketbooks by a discussion of the subject of giving, but because it is a subject that is dealt with in the word of God that we spend our time studying this particular subject.

There are those that think that the church can be financed just any way and that just any way that is not outside the law, and sometimes even outside the law, as long as it is a good fund raising method. There are those that think that the church should be financed in such ways. It is not uncommon to hear of a church that is raising money by bingo. Well, that is outside the law in the state of Alabama but maybe in some states it is lawful. Is this the way that God wants the church to be financed?

Up in Huntsville, Alabama, where I grew up, my father until recent years, was in the insulation business. He insulated many homes and he found out after a while that he was insulating a home for one of the churches up there. They were building homes and selling them. This was the way the church was financing their building program, their benevolent program and their evangelistic program. Is this the way that God wanted the church to function? Quite often there are those that have cake walks, there are those that have their little banquets and other ways. Sometimes there are those that sell donuts door to door, there are those that sell chances on automobiles or sell chances on shotguns or on quilts that they have made. There are those that have the idea maybe that the end justifies any means. Be aware that this principle will not work. We would not condone, for example, what was done in Corinth where the young women gave their bodies to the men who paid them and the money was used to promote the religion of that day. Certainly no one would think that this was a legitimate way that the church should be financed.

Does the Bible leave us in the dark as to how the church should finance its program of work? Well, it does not. In 48 words in the book of 1 Corinthians the Apostle Paul sets forth the perfect plan for giving. He says here, "Now concerning the collection for the saints, as I have given order to the churches of Galatia, ever so do ye: upon the first day of the week let every one of you lay by him in store, as God hath prospered him, that there be no gatherings when I come." (1 Corinthians 16:1-2)

First of all, we notice that the church is to be financed by the giving of its members, not through any business enterprise, not through any salesmanship promotion, but the church is to be financed by the free-will offering of its members on the first day of the week. This is spelled out in the word of God in this verse.

First, the perfect day of giving, "Upon the first day of the week...," Paul said. The first day of the week in Biblical terms refers to Sunday and upon every Sunday, he says God's people are to give. First we notice there Is the perfect day for giving the first day of the week. I know there are churches that think that every time they come together they have to take up a collection. This is not the way that the church was financed in New Testament times. There are emergency situations when this would be legitimate and acceptable. If a man's house burned down, for example, and an emergency arises, certainly it would not be wrong with God's people giving, but for the members to give every time they come together was not the way it was done in New Testament times, upon the first day of the week," this was something that was to be done especially.

God's perfect people, "let every one of you." There are some who say let the rich give. I will leave it up to Brother Jones or Brother Smith. They have more money than I have. Let them carry on the program of the church. But this was what God says, "Let everyone of you lay by him in store as God has prospered him." That is, man is to give according to his income, not a hit and miss situation, not as if God is the object of charity, not as if Christ has left it up to man's judgement alone; but he is to give as God has prospered him. If I have some income, a part of that should be used to carry on the work of the Lord. If we do not do this, the Lord's work will die upon the earth. That is the only way that the Gospel can be preached in all the world in an acceptable way, that is by everyone of the members of the Lord's family every Sunday giving a part of what he made during the week prior to that time as God has prospered him.

Some say if I give like this, I won't have anything left to feed my family and to take care of my family. Do you realize God blesses us in proportion to what we give to Him. The Bible says if a man sows sparingly, God will bless him sparingly; if a man sows bountifully, God will bless him bountifully. God cannot be out-given. As one man said when he was asked how do you feed all those children, he said, "I shovel out and the Lord shovels in and the Lord uses a bigger shovel than I do."

But you see, there would be a way for you never to have to mention the subject of giving. One time there was a man talking to a friend of his and he said, "You know, I used to have a son and that son was always wanting something. Dad, can I have this? Daddy, can I have that? Daddy, will you buy me this? But I don't hear that anymore because, you see, last year my son died."

It may seem that the church is always talking about giving. My friends, we can do away without ever having to give anything by letting the church die. Certainly we don't want to do this. Every Sunday, every Christian gives. This is the way the church is to be financed.

WILL A MAN ROB GOD?

We are living in a wonderful age. One of the advantages of life in our age is the fact that our money is pretty well secure in a bank. I know that in 1929, 30 and 31, many people lost their possessions. We are also very grateful that our banks are certainly more secure than they used to be. How many of us marveled at the old cowboy movies when someone would ride in on a horse with a gang behind him and they would take the money out of the bank. I believe I would be afraid to try to rob a bank today, wouldn't you, with all of the hidden cameras and everything else that is involved. A man would, indeed, be foolish to try to rob a bank. Yet I think some things are far worse than this and far more foolish is for a man to try to rob God. In Malachi we read of the people of God endeavoring to rob him. "Will a man rob God? Yet ye have robbed me. But ye say. Wherein have we robbed thee? In tithes and offerings." (Malachi 3:8) These people, the Hebrew people of old, had certainly been blessed by God. God had led them out of the land of Egypt where they had been enslaved for hundreds of years.

They got to the Red Sea and God told Moses to take his rod and put it over the Red Sea and the waters were divided and they marched through on dry land then their enemies were destroyed as they pursued after them. A little later on, they complained about the waters of Mamre and the Bible says that Moses prayed to God and God told him to cut down a tree and put it in the waters and as a result, the waters became sweet. God looked after these people by raining down bread from heaven. They didn't have to work while they were in the wilderness. God rained down manna from heaven. Later when they complained about not having meat, God caused quail to come down and they ate quail until the Bible says that quail ran out their nostrils. God certainly was good to these people and it seems strange, indeed, that they would ever want to rob him. Even stranger—those of us who are the recipients of blessings that the Israelites knew not of, and certainly we have been blessed far more abundantly than they could even imagine; yet sometimes we are guilty of robbing God. On today's telecast, I want to discuss with you the idea of a man robbing God. They raised the question in the long ago, "How will a man rob God?" and the response was that they robbed him in their tithes and offerings. What they were doing was not just simply omitting God entirely from their lives. What they actually were doing was bring the lame and sick lambs and offering them in their sacrifice. How do we rob God today? There are a number of ways:

Number one, we often rob God by not giving him our hearts. In Matthew 22, in response to a question asked by a lawyer, Jesus said,

"...Thou Shalt love the Lord thy God with all thy heart, and with all thy soul, and with all thy mind. (Matt. 22:37)

Jesus said one shall love God with all thy heart, not with a part of thy heart. When we do not give our heart totally, entirely and completely to God, we are guilty of robbing God—robbing him of our heart. God deserves to be number one in our life; yet how many of us have as the number one priority in our life the service to God? How many of us are putting little league baseball and many other things before service to God? "But seek ye first the kingdom of God, and his righteousness; and all these things shall be added unto you." (Matthew 6:33)

Yet it is difficult for us to commit our lives completely and totally to God. I think the real test comes when there is something that we would like to do and we know we have a Christian duty and a Christian responsibility and we chose to do that which we want rather than what God would have us to do. The real test of our devotion and dedication is that when there is something that God wants us to do that goes against the grain.

That is what happened in the life of Abraham. God told Abraham to take that son Isaac, that son that he had waited so long to have, and offer him as a sacrifice, Abraham got up early the next morning and went on the way. He went to the point of actually having the knife raised to kill his own son and God said now I know that you believe. Now he knew Abraham trusted him entirely. Now he knew he had given his life completely to him. Because of this, Abraham is the only man specifically designated in all the Bible as the man who is the friend of God.

Another way that we rob God, in addition to robbing God of our heart, is that we rob God of our bodies. In the proper use of our bodies.

"What? Know ye not that your body is the temple of the Holy Ghost which is in you, which ye have of God, and ye are not your own? For ye are bought with a price: therefore glorify God in your body, and in your spirit, which are God's" (1 Corinthians 6:19-20)

"I beseech you therefore, brethren, by the mercies of God, that ye present your bodies a living sacrifice, holy, acceptable unto God, which is your reasonable service. And be not conformed to This world: but be ye transformed by the renewing of your mind, that ye may prove what is that good, and acceptable, and perfect will of God." (Romans 12:1-2)

Are our bodies really given to God? Have we really dedicated our bodies in the service of God? If we saw a duck wander into the studio—at least an animal that looked like a duck, walked like a duck, was associated with other ducks—we would say undoubtedly that is a duck. When we see Christians who are acting like the world, who are dressing like the world, who associate with people of the world, whose thoughts are of the world, and whose appetites are the appetites of worldly people then we can see these people are not acting like Christian people act, they are acting like worldly people.

Do you give your body in service to God? What about those of you who are guilty of the misuse and improper use of your bodies, such things as drinking. In 1 Corinthians 6:9-10, Paul says that no drunkard will be permitted to enter into the kingdom of heaven. Actually the text that we started with, 1 Corinthians 6:19-20, was in a setting with those who are guilty of the sin of fornication and he said you are not to commit fornication. How widespread fornication and adultery are in the American society; yet he said you have no right to engage in that practice because you are not your own, you are bought with a price, you belong to the Lord—therefore you glorify God in your bodies and in your spirit which are his.

Thirdly and finally, we mention to you that we rob God often of worship. God wants us to worship him.

"God is a Spirit: and they that worship him must worship him in spirit and in truth." (John 4:24)

Do you worship God? Somebody says, what is worship? Worship is paying homage to a divine being or a being that we believe greater than we are; but true worship is worship that is dictated on the pages of God's word. God has specified how he wants to be worshipped.

"But in vain they do worship me, teaching for doctrines the commandments of men." (Matthew 15:9)

It is impossible to worship God acceptably unless we follow the dictates of his divine will. Are you worshipping God as he has commanded in his word or are you following the traditions of men? We must not follow men. I don't know of any man that is right one hundred percent of the time. I don't know any man that I have ever known in my years of life that was a perfect man. Because we are men of imperfection, no man is worthy to follow. Therefore in our worship, we must not follow the teaching of some church, which simply is composed of people who are sinners and who often transgress the law of God and fall short of what God wants them to be; but we must follow the commandments of the Bible in our worship.

What about those of you viewing our telecast today? Will you be worshipping God? Will some of you stay home today rather than worship him? God gave us days on which we can earn our livelihood and he asked that one day be given to him in specific service and worship. That is the day of worship, the first day of the week—Sunday. Yet there are those that steal this day from God.

"Not forsaking the assembling of ourselves together, as the manner of some is; but exhorting one another: and so much the more, as ye see the day approaching." (Hebrews 10:25)

What about you? Are you going to forsake the assembly today? You may say. Brother Jerry, I can't get out this morning. I have other commitments. What about tonight? What about the evening service? Can you come and worship God tonight? Can you sing songs of praise to his divine name? Can you give of your money and can you engage in the observance of the Lord's Supper and engage in Bible Study and prayer with those who are men and women of like faith, a common faith? What a grand and glorious privilege we have of worshipping God.

We need to worship him. We need to worship because worship will help us to be better. Worship doesn't help God. Worship is for our benefit and you will be a better person if you worship him. Your life will be richer. You will be able to meet the temptations and problems. You will be fortified against life. Come and worship God today.

LECTURESHIPS

Dad may have been at his best at lectureships. He really got geared up for them. To have the opportunity to influence those who would then go out an influence others was important to him.

The following lessons are ones presented at the lectureships of Pepperdine (1963), Harding (1973), Alabama Christian College (1971) and Freed-Hardeman (1983 and 1985).

J & D

THE PREACHER'S NEED TO STUDY

PEPPERDINE LECTURES

1963

A few months ago in Huntsville, Alabama my sister-in-law told of a certain man who had never been to church. His wife begged and pled with him continually, but he stubbornly refused. Finally because of her persistence he agreed to go—one time. The preacher in the denomination they attended felt the need to call a meeting with his board of stewards to discuss some important matters. He made the following announcement at the close of services: "I want to meet with all the board immediately upon our dismissal." To the utter amazement of this group, the man who had never been to church before, stayed after services with them. Finally after much painful delay, the preacher courageously asked why he had stayed. "Well, you said for all the bored to meet after services and I'll guarantee you there wasn't anybody here any more bored than me." I have been asked to speak for the next few minutes on, "The Preacher's Need to Study." Certainly one reason he needs to study is to keep his hearers from being bored. I trust that as we reason together none of you will be bored. Paul instructed the young preacher Timothy, "Study to show thyself approved unto God, a workman that needeth not to be ashamed, rightly dividing the word of truth." (2 Timothy 2:15) This verse emphasizes the need for zeal, haste, effort and earnest desire to present ourselves approved. The word "study" in the verse is not limited to a study of the Bible, nor of nature, nor human nature, but in giving diligence to meet with approval, care of study is necessary.

Personal Benefit

The preacher needs to study for his own benefit. In our calorie-conscious-age we must never go on a starvation diet from the word of God. The absolute necessity for God's children to feast on His word is stressed throughout the Bible. "And he humbled thee, and suffered thee to hunger, and fed thee with manna, which thou knowest not, neither did thy fathers know; that he might make thee know that man doth not live by bread only, but by every word that proceedeth out of the mouth of the Lord doth man live." (Deuteronomy 8:3) "Neither have I gone back from the commandment of his lips; I have esteemed the word of his mouth more than my necessary food." (Job 23:12) The Psalmist said, "How sweet are thy words unto my taste! Yea sweeter than honey to my mouth." (Psalm 119:103) The weeping prophet in his emotional manner stated, "Thy words were found, and I did eat them; and thy word was unto me the joy and rejoicing of mine heart: for I am called by thy name, O Lord God of hosts." (Jerermiah 15:16)

Not only was Jesus the first in the New Testament to teach the value of eating proper spiritually, He used it frequently. "Blessed are they which do hunger and thirst after righteousness: for they shall be filled." (Matthew 5:6) Three times he admonished Peter to feed his people.

Peter did not forget the figure, "As new born babes, desire the sincere milk of the word, that ye may grow thereby..." (1 Peter 2:2)

About five months ago a man from New York was involved in an automobile accident near us and placed in the Lister Hill Hospital in Hamilton. His leg injuries had caused a long confinement and gave occasion for us to talk frequently. Recently he was telling me of some of the doubts he had regarding the accuracy of the Bible. A nurse had entered while he was talking and as he finished said, "Robert, the old boogeyman is making you talk like that, you better put away every appearance of evil." When she left, Robert said,"Mr. Jenkins that attitude is the very reason why I cannot believe in God— Christians are afraid to think."

Faith does not fear investigation. There is no merit in stupidity. Charles S. Horne in his lecture at Yale said: "...there is nothing in Holy Writ to warrant the assumption that a man is likely to be more spiritual if he is an ignoramus; or that prophetic power in the pulpit essentially attaches to the preacher whose heart is full and whose head is empty."

A preacher needs to study lest his mind deteriorate by lack of use. Shortly after Bobby Morrow had performed out-standing feats in the Olympics, I heard him tell of the champion hammer-thrower. Bobby said he looked almost deformed. His right arm, because of its continual use, was a picture of manly-muscle, but his left arm, because it was so seldom used was slender and weak. Our minds are just like this. When we fail to use them in study they become weak and frail.

The Hebrews writer states the case: "For when the time ye ought to be teachers, ye have need that one teach you again which be the first principles of the oracles of God; and are become such as have need of milk, and not of strong meat. For every one that useth milk is unskillful in the word of righteousness: for he is a babe. But strong meat belongeth to them that are of full age, even those who by reason of use have their senses exercised to discern both good and evil." (Hebrews 5:12-14)

Study allows the preacher to see himself and his work as God sees them. James describes God's word as a mirror. This will do away with an over estimation of our own merits and make us conscious that the strength of God is made known in our weakness.

To Benefit Others

A second major reason for the need for preachers to study is to benefit others. First in teaching the truth and that only. A preacher is to speak as the oracle of God. If he alters the gospel the anathema of heaven rest on him. Neither addition nor subtraction meets with God's approval.

I remember the first year I took Greek tearing up several sermon outlines because I had missed the true meaning of the text. Perhaps an even more popular practice is a failure to bring to light some of the real beauties of God's scheme in redeeming man.

We are living in an age which radio, television, and better schooling opportunities have raised the expectation of the hearers. As listeners no longer will permit a speaker to say: "I seen," or other grammatical errors, he expects him to be better informed in all areas than ever before.

I do not mean by this statement that our lessons should become orations to be applauded rather than a message to be believed and acted upon, but they should be the best we can give—intellectually and every other way and this is impossible unless there is devoted study.

Parkhurst stated: "There is no sort of knowledge, whether of things celestial or terrestrial, of things divine or human, that cannot be utilized to the effectiveness of pulpit discourse."

Henry Ward Beecher said, "A minister ought to be the best informed man on the face of the earth."

You and I preach the necessity of study almost weekly. We cannot afford to ask others to do that which we will not. We may benefit others by setting the proper example in study.

In January of this year I sat in the study of Brother Gus Nichols talking with him about the need preachers have to study. He talked of the same problem which others have experienced. The cries which take one away from study. I marveled once again at his knowledge of God's word and human nature. Then his secret which we already knew came into the conversation. Brother Nichols said, "I try to study at least five hours every day." I went home with renewed determination to study more. My point is—study begets study. When we study we will encourage others.

To Please God

All of the things we have been suggesting could be summed up in our final simple point, preachers need to study to show our appreciation to God.

Please notice the frequency of this command: Deuteronomy 6:6-9; Nehemiah 8:8; Proverbs 3:13; Proverbs 4:5; Proverbs 15:14; Proverbs 23:23; John 8:31,32; Ephesians 5:17; 1 Peter 3:15; and 2 Peter 1:5-10.

I challenge you to study more. Brother Baxter in his great book, The Heart of the Yale Lectures, lists the qualities most desirable in preachers as seen by the speakers in the 71 year history of the Yale Lectures. He informs us that the importance of study and the acquisition of knowledge was given stronger emphasis than any other characteristic except character.

Conclusion

In 1958 in Nashville, Tennessee I heard for the first time of an incident the old pioneer preachers use to tell in challenging their audience to do more for the Lord.

There was a little one-room school that was having a difficult time keeping a teacher. A young man fresh from college applied for the position. The school board tried to discourage him, but to no avail. On the first day the room was filled with eager students whose ages ranged from 6 to 20 or over. To their delight the new teacher started by telling them they could make the rules and he would write them on the board. It was not long before three boards were full of rules that the students had made.

The teacher next stated that rules were no good unless there was some means of enforcing them. George, the largest boy in class spoke from the back, "I think anybody caught violating a rule should receive 10 licks from the paddle." All the students readily agreed.

Three weeks passed and then Jim, the runt of the class, was caught stealing another's lunch and violating one of the rules. The students gathered eagerly around to watch him punished.

The teacher instructed him to remove his coat. To their surprise he had on no shirt. When the teacher began to question it was revealed that his mother had died. He had no shirt because his father just couldn't get the jobs finished. He had taken the lunch to feed his younger brother and sister at home.

A hush filled the room. But still the rules must be enforced. George spoke, "I'd like to take the whipping for Jim." On the fifth lick the paddle broke and Jim went over and put his arm around George in thanks. Jesus took the whipping we deserved—let us thank Him by diligence in studying and obeying His will.

FATAL EXPERIMENTS: DRINK AND DRUGS

ALABAMA CHRISTIAN COLLEGE LECTURES
1971

Our Dad was what some people call a teetotaler. As far as we know, he never took a single drink of anything alcoholic. Not only did he refrain from alcohol, but he also discouraged drunkenness and even social drinking for everyone who claimed to be a Christian. One of the reasons Dad felt so strongly about drinking was because he saw families destroyed, friendships ruined, and souls pulled away from God because of alcohol.

In this lecture delivered during the Alabama Christian College lectures in 1971, Dad presented a thoughtful study of the Danger of Drinking and Drugs. We include it here in hopes that more preachers will not be deterred from preaching the Word of God on this subject by culture, fame, or fortune.

J & D

It was 8 o'clock when I left the building, my wife seated in the front seat beside me; following behind was a new family who had just moved into Birmingham and we had invited them over for some refreshments. You turn down Division Avenue and standing in the middle of the street I saw something I never would have believed possible. I never thought I would see anything like this in Birmingham. Standing there, waving for us to stop was a woman with no clothes. After phoning for help, we discovered that the lady was high on drugs.

Though this was an embarrassing experience, this time the lady got off lightly because all she did was to expose herself in an embarrassing situation. Many are not so fortunate; some jump out of windows, others became living vegetables for the rest of their life, and some affect unborn generations.

The topic for this hour - "Fatal Experiments-Drink and Drugs". The Bible sets forth the principle that we are not to abuse our bodies and to do so is a sinful practice (1 Corinthians 6:19-20). Instead of such abuse, we are to use our bodies to the glory of God. Paul declared, "No drunkard shall inherit the kingdom of God" (1 Corinthians 6:9-10). This would include drunkenness in all forms, whether brought about by alcohol or drugs. To the Roman Christians, Paul stated in Romans 13:13, "Walk honestly...not in rioting and drunkenness". Once he gave the prohibition, "Be not drunk with wine" (Ephesians 5:18).

The history of drink is dark and bleak. Centuries ago when the grace of God so brightly shown, sparing Noah and his family from their evil surroundings. Noah was filled with such gratitude, perhaps he thought he would never do anything to the disfavor of God. As so often is the case, only a short time later we read of his planting a vineyard and of the terrible sin of Ham when he saw his father In this drunken condition (Genesis 9:21)

Nabal was so drunk that his wife, Abigail, dared not tell him of the mercy she had extracted from David. Ten days later, the Bible graphically describes his death, stating that his heart was turned to stone (1 Samuel 25:36)

A third Incident In the bleak history of drink occurs In the life of King David. After David had committed the terrible sin with Bathsheba, in an attempt to cover up this black sin, he sent for Uriah, Bathsheba's husband. David, realizing the power of drink, endeavored to hide his Immorality by getting Uriah drunk and extending him a furlough with his wife. His plot failed (2 Samuel 11:13).

Drink became the ally of Ahasuerus as he endeavored to get Vashti to parade before his men Immodestly clad (Esther 1:10). All of these examples indicate that those under the influence of drink will do things which, when sober, they would not do.

It must be admitted by any Bible reader, that no drunkard will be saved. There is a growing group within the church who condone occasionally what is called social drinking. Three passages are often introduced to prove such drinking permissible: first, Jesus turned water into wine (John 2); second, the difference made in the qualifications of elders and deacons (1 Timothy 3); and finally, Paul's statement to Timothy to take a little wine for his illness.

In response to this, let it be noted that there is a tremendous difference in culture, water conditions, and in the drink itself. Even granting that the wine referred to in all of the above scriptures would produce inebriation, there is still a vast difference in such wine and the distilled liquor which plagues our society. The case against drinking of any intoxicating beverage can be made brief and, yet, powerful.

Two years ago while I was in a meeting in Chicago, Illinois, the local preacher drove me down a street. I saw, not one or two, but scores of men in the middle of the day out cold on the hard sidewalks. In May of 1969, in Belize, British Honduras, I saw the nauseating sight of a man who had become inebriated and was lying in his own regurgitation.

No one wants to be like one of these bums. No one sets out to become a confirmed alcoholic and yet one out of every 15 social drinkers becomes an alcoholic, and one out of every nine becomes a social drinker. If you never become an alcoholic, you still have the responsibility to guard your influence and to use it to the glory of God. The social drinker, influence wise, is more detrimental than the drunkard. Think of it, brethren, we have those in the church who are condoning practices which prohibit the use of one's body to the glory of God and by no stretch of the imagination can it be said that their acts bring glory to the name of God. (Matthew 5:16)

The Effect of Alcohol on the Digestive System

A second argument against social drinking is the effect that alcohol has on the digestive system. Alcohol in small amounts, leads to an increase in the flow of gastric juices and contractions of the stomach. It is one of the few substances which may be absorbed into the blood stream through the wall of the stomach without being digested. Continued use may lead to the inflammation of the esophagus, stomach and intestine.

Chronic irritation prevents the stomach from performing and this effects loss of appetite, trouble in digestion and nausea often occurs. Among heavy drinkers, cirrhosis of the liver is common. Alcohol does provide 200 calories per ounce but offers no minerals, vitamins or protein.

Although it does produce some energy, it produces so many harmful effects that it cannot be regarded in a class with such fbod as milk, meat, fruit and vegetables.

I again remind you of Paul's admonition that our body is to be used to the glory of God. I raise the question, how can we be heeding this admonition, realizing the effect alcohol has on our digestive system?

It's Effect on the Brain

As bad as the effect alcohol has on our digestive system, what it does to the brain is even worse. In the first stage, even small quantities effect the cerebrum. This means a decrease in social responsibility and judgment and removes inhibitions. In the second stage, the functions controlled by the cerebellum are effected. Psychological and physiological changes can be observed in the area of motor and sensory reaction time. Walking, talking, hearing, driving and clumsiness takes the place of precision. In the third place, the medula is affected, resulting in stupor, unconsciousness and commas. Finally paralysis of the center which controls breathing results in death.

Recently Dr. Melvin H. Khisely, Professor of Anatomy at the Medical University of South Carolina, and a team of scientists conducted experiments which concluded that every time a person takes a few drinks of an alcoholic beverage, even a few beers at a social function, permanent damage is done to his brain. Red blood cells, as you know, are the agent that carries oxygen to the brain. A diminishing of this oxygen for only a few minutes can do permanent damage and to interrupt this oxygen for ten minutes is lethal. Dr. Knisely and his group showed that when one drinks even a small quantify, that the red blood cells become sticky and adhere together, diminishing the oxygen received into the brain.

Dr. Otto Haug of the Psychiatry Department at Frederikstad in Norway injected chemicals into the brain which showed that alcohol brought about a decrease of brain tissue. His conclusion was that beer drinking does as much damage as drinking whiskey.

Drugs

Drugs can be classified either as addicting or habit forming and whether they are a stimulate or a depressant. Addicting drugs affect users differently, but all addicting drugs give rise to one or more of the following conditions. First, dependence on the drug. This can be either emotional or psychological. In either case, such dependence is known as habituation. Second, tolerance to the drugs. By tolerance, we mean the building up in the user of a condition whereby each successive dose has a diminishing effect and the user Is obligated to increase the dosage to get the same effect. Third, physical dependence on the drugs. Addicts develop rapidly in opiates such as morphine and heroin and slow as in the case of barbiturates or sleeping pills.

Opiates and barbiturates produce all three of the above effects. Marijuana, bromides and amphetamines produce only emotional dependence. Habit-forming drugs according to the Bureau of Narcotics, can be listed as coffee, tea, chocolate, cola drinks and tobacco. In these, the dosage need not be increased for the same effect and one can stop or reduce the use without experiencing withdrawal illness.

The discussion of drugs will be divided in this lecture into two parts. First, the narcotic, which is much more dangerous but less accessible. Second, a discussion of what I consider to be the most dangerous drugs because of their accessibility,

1. Opium: the air-dried, milky exudate obtained from the capsule of the opium or sleep poppy. Its most active principle is morphine. It is a white odorless powder with a bitter taste and it controls the central nervous system. It would be used to control pain.

2. Heroin: this Is another narcotic which we have heard a great deal about. It is the most dangerous derivative of morphine and has more effect on the respiration. It is often sniffed or injected into the veins. It makes troubles roll off one's mind.

3: Cocaine: obtained from the coca tree found in Peru, Chile, and Bolivia. It is one of the oldest and most dangerous drugs. Prolonged use causes a persecution delusion.

Recently Jerry Crabtree, who last year was the president of the Alabama Sheriff Association, told of the depths to which one sinks in fulfillment of their craving of these drugs. He told of seeing a young boy cut off his heels and flush them down the commode in order that they would take him to a hospital where he could receive morphine. It is heroin which causes many to sell their bodies, to steal, and even to kill to satisfy their desires.

We next turn our attention to the drugs which are more available.

First, Marijuana. The source of Marihuana is the female Indian hemp plant. It grows practically all over the United States. Marijuana is referred to as pot, tea, grass, weed, Mary Jane, etc. Most often in this country, it is rolled into cigarettes called reefers, joints, moochas, sticks, etc. Marijuana enters the bloodstream and affects one's mood and thinking. If often causes one to become talkative, loud, unsteady or drowsy. One, under it's influence, has no conception of distance or time. One cigarette can make one feel silly. After four cigarettes, one's perceptive changes, colors become brighter and hearing seems keener. After ten cigarettes, one begins to have hallucinations.

In addition to the sin of abuse of one's body, there is also the fact that one who uses or is even in possession of Marijuana, is outside the law of our land, consequently outside the law of God. (Rom. 13)

In 1970 a new federal law was passed which makes even the possession of Marijuana, the penalty of one year in prison and/ or $500 for the first offense. For selling Marijuana, the penalty is 15 years and/or $25,000 fine.

Up and Down Drugs

A second culprit in the list of drugs is called up and down drugs. Amphetamines, or stimulants, are often used by weight watchers. There is a tendency to cut down on food and there is also an increase in heart rate. There is a rise in blood pressure. Pupils are dilated and the mouth becomes dry. Amphetamines are referred to as pep pills, bennies or speed. The real danger is that is presses one beyond their safe physical endurance. A mixture with alcohol often causes death, as in the case of Dorothy Kilgalen.

Barbiturates are sedatives and a depressant. It decreases heart beat and lowers the blood pressure. Barbiturates are referred to as barb or goof balls. They are dangerous because they are addictive.

Hallucinogens

The third and final drug we will discuss is LSD. The chemical name is D-lysergic acid diethylamide. Recently a college student at one of our colleges in Birmingham told of making LSD in a chemistry lab.

One ounce of LSD can make 300,000 average doses. It can be concealed which is evident by people getting high on LSD by licking the back of a stamp. The real danger of LSD is that it often causes panic. Secondly, it creates paranoia. Some have felt that the world was against them.

Then 72 hours after the drug had worn off, a third danger is in its recurrence. There have been incidents when people, many months later, went on a trip similar to the one they had experienced when they actually used LSD. Fourth is that it causes birth defects.

Reasons for Drug Use

What causes young people to use drugs? First, children grow up seeing parents who are dependent on drugs. Second, the influence of rock music. The lyrics of these songs often suggest running away from home and finding a friend (drugs) to solve every problem. Often those who sing such songs are users of drugs. Life Magazine reported that before the Beatles received Britain's highest award from the Queen herself, they went into the men's room and got high on drugs. Third, advertisement; television offers every kind of pill to solve every kind of problem. Advertising makes drugs seem common place and thereby destroying the fear of the unknown. Fourth, advocates such as Timothy Leary, a Harvard Professor, and Margaret Mead who said if she were 16, she would be smoking marijuana.

The key factor of the intake of drugs and drink is, as the name of this lecture suggests, experiments. It is young people seeking something. Perhaps God's word anticipated that drunkenness would be a substitute for something our generation is seeking. Paul stated in Ephesians 5:18 that we are not to be filled with wine, but be filled with the spirit. From this verse it is obvious that the acceptance of God's word displaces the need for wine.

The wise man Solomon stated in Song of Solomon 1:4, "We will be glad and rejoice in thee, we will remember thy love more than wine, the upright love thee". In Isaiah 5:11-12, there is a contrast made regarding the work of the Lord and following strong drink. There is a vivid description of the problems developing out of strong drink in Isaiah 28:1-7. In Isaiah 55:1, there is a comparison made of the blessing of Christianity and that which man would consider good living.

Young people, Christianity is not restrictive in the sense that it deprives one of the fuller life. In fact, it is only in Christ that one can find the abundant life (John 10:10). Christianity offers one the true values of life and can give to each of you a real purpose in living.

I appeal to you to dedicate your life completely to Christ and there will be no need for drugs in any form.

THE MAN WITH A
BURNING HEART
HARDING LECTURES
1973

Dad spoke on just about every major lectureship in the brotherhood. He never pushed himself on people to "get" invitations but he seemed to always appreciate them. In 1973, he spoke a couple of times on the Harding University Lectures.

One of his lessons at Harding was delivered between the lessons delivered by two very close friends, Jimmy Allen, and Jerry Jones. The three of them had been very close friends during their early years of preaching and remained close until Dad passed away. Dad told the story that when he spoke, he made a comment about "a rose between two thorns." Following his lesson, when brother Allen spoke, he said it was more like "a piece of bologna between two pieces of bread!" Dad enjoyed that exchange very much.

His assignments were lessons that were right in his "wheelhouse!" One lesson was titled, "Friendship Evangelism." The other was this lesson, "The Man With the Burning Heart." It is an outstanding message about the heart of Paul. Our prayer is that this sermon will encourage all of us to develop a "Holy Heartburn" for our Lord.

J & D

In one of the most familiar and challenging statements in all the Bible, Paul affirms,

"I am debtor both to the Greeks, and to the Barbarians; both to the wise, and to the unwise. So, as much as in me is, I am ready to preach the gospel to you that are at Rome also... For I am not ashamed of the gospel of Christ: for it is the power of God unto salvation to every one that believeth; to the Jew first, and also to the Greek. For therein is the righteousness of God revealed from faith to faith: as it is written, The just shall live by faith." (Romans 1:14-17)

There are two words that are extremely interesting in this passage; the words "prothumon" and "euangelisasthai." They are translated into the English language by seven words. These seven words are, "I am ready to preach the gospel." One of these words, the word "prothumon" is from the word "thumos." Albert Smith said this word could correctly be translated "hot anger." Thayer says it means "boiling up" or to "heat," and is akin to the word that is often translated in the Bible by the term "fire." So Paul is saying in Romans 1:15 that he is on fire for God; he is on fire to preach the gospel of the Lord Jesus Christ. The term "fire" is often employed in the word of God to denote the intensity and dedication of the men who were serving the Lord. For example, Jeremiah said, "Then I said, I will not make mention of him, nor speak any more in his name. But his word was in mine heart as a burning fire shut up in my bones, and I was weary with forbearing, and I could not stay." (Jeremiah 29:9) Here Jeremiah said he had tried to stop preaching. Perhaps he was weary; perhaps he was discouraged; perhaps he didn't think he was accomplishing any good. But he said, "When I resigned my

job, when I got ready to quit preaching, the word of God was
like a fire burning in my bones and I was weary with forbearing
and I could not stay." Jeremiah was saying that he had to preach.
He couldn't do anything else but preach. Vance Havner called
him a man with a holy fever, a preacher running a spiritual
temperature. In John 5:35 the Bible says, in speaking of John the
Baptist, "He was a burning and a shining light ... " How
interesting it is that the word of God describes the life of John
the Baptist, that way-preparer for the Lord, that voice crying in
the wilderness, as a man who was burning for God.

In Psalms 38:3 the Psalmist said, "My heart was hot within
me; while I was musing the fire burned: then spake I with my
tongue." Once an aged gospel preacher said to a younger gospel
preacher, "Boys, if you can do anything else, don't preach." I
think that is what David had in mind when he said, "My heart
was hot within me; while I was musing the fire burned: then
spake I with my tongue." Jesus said in Luke 12:49, "I am come to
send fire on the earth: and what will I, if it be already kindled?"
Perhaps everyone present this afternoon is familiar with that
passage found in Luke 24 :32. Cleopas and another disciple had
just left the presence of Jesus. "And they said one to another,
Did not our heart burn within us ... ?

Several years ago, Brother Basil Overton had an article in
The World Evangelist in which he pointed out the fact that all
of us need to be on fire for God, but we need to be set on fire in
the proper way. We do not need to be as the wood in the
fireplace without any flame, nor as a forest fire burning out of
control; but as a blow torch-a controlled fire. These two men
who had conversation with Jesus said as they were talking, and

he explained to us the scriptures, "Our heart burn within us." We need to be set on fire by the scriptures.

Paul said, "I have a burning within me to tell the good news of Jesus Christ." Paul said in Acts 20 :24 to the elders of Ephesus on the little isle of Miletus, that "none of these things moved me." "These things," Paul said, "did not set me on fire." Paul had been expelled from the city of Antioch in Pisidia. Paul had been stoned in Lystra and left for dead. Paul had been beaten and with bleeding wounds he was put in the stocks in prison in Philippi. But Paul said, "None of these things moved me." He could not be moved by persecution. Paul could not be moved by false teachers. He said, "Do I seek to please God or men?" (Gal 1 : 10) He said in Galatians 2 that we "gave them space, no, not for an hour." Paul could not be moved even by his friends·. He said in Galatians 2:11-13 that Peter was to blame and he had to rebuke him to his face.

Here was a man who could not be easily moved. He was a stubborn man. He could not be moved by being whipped; he could not be moved by being beaten; he could not be moved by false teachers that would attack him. He could not be moved even by his friends for he was a stubborn man. Ladies and gentlemen, I am convinced that there was something that set Paul on fire, and this afternoon we do not want to talk about these things simply in a factual way, but we should make application into our own hearts and into our own lives. These things that moved Paul surely must be able to move us today if we are the right kind of people. Five things motivated him; five things made the great Apostle Paul the great man that he was. These are mentioned with the hope that it also might move us and motivate us to be more dedicated and devoted servants of the Lord. Each one of these things will begin with a "c" in order to help us remember them.

First of all there was the call of Jesus Christ from above. In Acts 26, Paul was recounting his conversion before old King Agrippa. He said to Agrippa that he had permission and authority from the chief priests and that he went to every synagogue often to persecute the Christians. He didn't go occasionally; he didn't go once a year; but he went often, and he said he also compelled those to blaspheme the name of Jesus. He tried by persecution to get people to recant their faith and to take the name of Jesus in vain. He said he traveled not only to the local cities but also to strange cities and those that were far removed. It was while he was on the way to one of these strange cities, the city of Damascus, that about noon a bright light, brighter than the noonday sun, shone round about and he fell to the ground, along with all of those with him. A voice from heaven said, "Saul, Saul, why persecutest thou me? It is hard for thee to kick against the pricks." This voice said he had appeared to make him a minister and a witness to bear my name among the Gentiles and Paul said he was not disobedient to that heavenly vision. So the apostle said he had a call from God. Some time ago I read about a certain sergeant who was instructed by his captain to take a certain hill, and he argued with his captain. He was called before the officers and court martialed. As first they wanted to shoot him but later his sentence was changed to life imprisonment. At the time the article was written, it was said that the young man was still in jail. He was in prison for disobeying the orders of a military superior.

I wonder how the Lord must think of us when we are not obedient to the heavenly call that we have received. In Mark 16:15 Jesus said, "Go ye into the world, and preach the gospel to every creature." In Matthew 28 :19 he said "Go ye therefore, and teach all nations..." There are about four reasons why we are disobedient to the orders of our Captain.

In the first place, we are not evangelizing the world because we are just too indifferent. We are really not concerned about the man who is lost in sin. We will just have to confess that we are too indifferent or we have something more interesting to us rather than carry the marching orders of the Lord Jesus Christ.

In the second place, we are too pre-occupied. We have so many activities going on that we do not have time to get on with the Lord's work. A gospel preacher told me some time ago that he spent about eight hours every day in his office and the only persons that he tried to teach the gospel were those that came in and invited him to study with them. I don't believe this is carrying out the commission of our Lord, and I am sure you don't either.

In the next place, we might as well admit that we are too lazy. Brethren, we are just too lazy to do what the Lord had told us to do~to go and preach the gospel to those that are lost in sin.

And perhaps, in the fourth place, we really don't know. Yet, if we really have the love that we should have for the lost, we will learn how. I know a man who lives in the northwestern part of Arkansas. Every time I have ever been in that area for a gospel meeting I have the opportunity to go out and visit with him. I have always learned something from this old tenant farmer, a share cropper. He doesn't own an acre of land. He doesn't own a house, but he is concerned about the lost. I said to him one day, "Brother, why is it that you know so much about reaching the lost with the gospel?" Then he took me in and showed me his library. About every book on personal work that I have ever read or heard of was there in his library. I am saying to you that if we really want to, we can carry out the commission. So Paul was a man on fire for God because of that call that he had from above.

In the second place there was the crowd around Paul. Not only the call and orders that he had from the Lord Jesus, but there was the crowd around him.

"When I say unto the wicked, o wicked man, thou shalt surely die; if thou dost not speak to warn the wicked from his way, that wicked man shall die in his iniquity; but his blood will I require at thine hand. Nevertheless, if thou warn the wicked of his way to turn from it; if he do not turn away from his way, he shall die in his iniquity; but thou hast delivered thy soul." (Ezekiel 33:8-9)

So Paul said, "I am a debtor." Paul, do you owe somebody some money? No. Paul, in what sense are you a debtor? I am a debtor because I have been commissioned to preach the gospel and have been given the grace and opportunity to preach the unsearchable riches to those that are lost in sin; therefore, that makes me a debtor. Paul was a debtor to all men.

Suppose today that you are in a ship, and another ship nearby went down and there were life preservers on the ship you are on and there were people all around you drowning. Let me ask you a question. Do you have any obligation to that man that is in the ocean drowning? Do you say, "It is not my fault that the ship sank on which they were traveling?" Would you say you feel no obligation? The very fact hat you were on the ship and safe, and you have some room on the ship, and you have some life preservers makes you a debtor. Paul felt this debt in the same way. So we need to feel keenly the debt that we owe to those that are lost.

Once a preacher taught an old man the gospel. Some time after his obedience the old man lay dying. In sorrow the preacher stood by his bedside. How thrilling it was for him to hear the old brother's final words, "When I get to heaven, I'm going to tell the Lord about you." A missionary was begged by the chief from a small African village to tell his people of Christ. The missionary did not have time. As he departed, the chief cried, "I'm going to tell the Lord on you." Which will it be for us? Will someone tell the Lord on us or about us?

In the third place, there was the crown before Paul. "For what is our hope, or joy, or crown of rejoicing? Are not even ye in the presence of our Lord Jesus Christ at his coming? For ye are our glory and joy." (1 Thessalonians 2:19-20)

Paul, what is the reason you have for a better life? What is your expectation of joy and what is your crown of rejoicing? Listen to his answer. "For ye are our glory and joy." Paul would say to you that the crown that he was seeking was the soul winner's crown. The brethren in Thessalonica whom he had the opportunity to teach comprised his crown. When would they be that crown that he would wear? When the Lord came, and when we would be all together in the presence of the Lord, this would be his joy and his hope and his crown. So I am convinced that Paul is saying to us that we need to want to wear a crown.

All of us have been thrilled to watch as Americans win gold medals at the Olympics. Who of you does not feel a sense of personal exaltation at the strains of the "Star Spangled Banner?" Many of you have been singled out for personal honors. But think of the greatest honor of all-the honor of wearing the soul winner's crown. When we can look about us and know that because of our love, concern, care, and willingness to be spent for Christ that there will be those who are spending eternity in the presence of the Lord, we know that earthly honors wax pale in comparison to this feeling of a job well done. I submit to you, my friends, that Paul was motivated as, a man on fire for God because of the crown that was above him.

Fourthly there was the catastrophe below him. Paul said,"Knowing the terror of the Lord, we persuade men." Paul could never forget how horrible it would be for a man to be lost in hell. May we refresh our memory for just a few moments. The Bible vividly describes what it is like to be lost.

Our Lord talked more about the confines of torment than anyone else who had anything to say about the subject. The Lord spoke often about Gehenna. He used the term eleven of the twelve times it occurs in the New Testament. He used it, not only to motivate us to fear being lost in hell, but also that we might encourage others not to spend eternity there.

The Bible describes hell as a place of fire. In Matthew 25:41, it is referred to as everlasting fire. In Matthew 13:41, it is called a furnace of fire. In Mark 9:44, it is referred to as unquenchable fire. In Revelation 20:14-15, the Bible describes hell as a lake of fire. I can think of many ways that I would rather die than burn to death. Some time ago on I-65 in Birmingham, Alabama, a couple in their late 60's era driving down the highway and their car was hit by another car from the rear and their car was set on fire. They were alive, pinned inside the car, and the door would not open. They screamed and hollered for somebody to get them out of that burning car. One man went over, according to the television newscast, and put his hand on the door but jerked his had away quickly because the door was too hot to touch. This old couple died begging someone to deliver them from that fire. The picture is still vivid for me, but that fire was put out. Paul didn't want anybody to die unprepared. He didn't want anybody to burn forever. So Paul was motivated to be a man on fire for God because of the catastrophe below.

Then there is the darkness in hell. There is something about darkness that we don't like. We would rather choose the day time to sit with the sick. We don't like to walk through a cemetery in the darkness of the night. There is something about the darkness that we just simply do not like. Some time ago, many miles from here I was in a gospel meeting. On Sunday afternoon, I was having lunch with a deacon and he said, "Do you want to go back into a coal mine?" We put on some old clothes and went back into the coal mine. After we had gone about two miles, he said "Turn out the lights." The darkness was so thick one could feel it-that is the lostness of the dark. I don't want to be lost in hell. I don't want to spend eternity in darkness. Then there are the sounds of hell-the weeping, not the crying of little children, but sobs of mature individuals, those old enough to understand what is involved in rebelling against God. Then there is the haunting memory when we will recall the opportunities we had to make our life right in the sight of God, when we shirked and wasted opportunities God had granted to us.

Then there will be the separation: mothers will be separated from daughters, and fathers will be separated from sons, and husbands from wives: one saved and the other lost. So Paul didn't want anybody to be lost. No wonder he could say to the elders at Ephesus that he "ceased not to warn you day and night with tears." He could say not only did he teach publicly, but also from house to· house. That which motivated Paul was not only the call from above and the crowd around him, not only the crown that was awaiting him in the judgment day, but also there was that catastrophe below that kept him going, perhaps tirelessly, until he could go on no more. So there was the catastrophe below.

Then finally I would mention to you there was the cross behind Paul. Paul was moved because of the cross behind him. Paul talked about the cross of Jesus often. He said, "I determine not to know anything among you save Jesus Christ and Him crucified." (1 Corinthians 2 :21.) He said, "God forbid that I should glory save in the cross of my Lord." (Galatians 6 :14.) He said in 2 Corinthians 5 :14 that the "love of Christ constraineth me." So if there is anything that ought to cause us to go away from this lectureship on fire for God, it ought to be the cross of our Lord Jesus Christ and we ought to think about it more. The cross must never become trite and meaningless to us but we ought to think about it every day of our lives in order to inspire us to do more and work for Jesus Christ.

More than 1900 years ago the Son of Glory left the splendors of being with God and came and dwelt among men. Though he was rich he became poor that we through his poverty might be made rich. When a certain scribe asked him, "Master, where dwelleth thou." He could only say, "The foxes have holes and the birds of the air have nests, but the Son of Man hath no where to lay His head." He was born of poor parentage indicated by the sacrifice of poverty made by Mary and Joseph. He grew up the son of a carpenter, and when he was still a young man, only 33 years of age, the acme of his abandonment became apparent. He had been rejected by his half-brothers and sisters. He had been turned down, run out of the little town of Nazareth where he had grown up when he tried to speak in the synagogue. He had been betrayed by one of the chosen twelve. He had been denied by Peter, and, according to Matthew 26 :56, he was forsaken by all of his disciples. Finally on the cross, He cried out, "My God, my God, why hast thou forsaken me." Martin Luther says the most difficult passage in all the Bible to understand is why would God abandon Christ when he needed Him so desperately. Why, at his darkest hour and his hour of greatest need, would God turn in the other direction? The answer is quite evident. The answer is because of you and me and that great love that he had for us. "God commended his love toward us that while we were yet sinners, Christ died for the ungodly." (Romans 5 :8.) We see Christ who "was made a little lower than the angels for the suffering of death, crowned with glory and honor that he for the grace of God might taste death for every man." (Hebrews 2:9)

The mob came after him in the Garden of Gethsemane. His disciples had fallen asleep three times and the third time he told them to sleep on. They came after him as though he were a hardened criminal. When he said, "I taught you daily in the temple" they fell back but they rushed after him again. He appeared before the priests and the fake High Priest, and finally He was taken to Pilate. Pilate sent Him over to Herod and Herod back to Pilate. Our Lord was abused. Everything sacred about our Lord was mocked and ridiculed. They made fun of the kingship of our Lord for they put a reed in his hand and a crown of thorns upon his head and said, "Hail, king of the Jews." Pilate had a superscription written in three languages, "This is the king of the Jews." So our Lord's kingship was mocked. The priestly role of our Lord was mocked as they wagged their heads and said he saved others but he cannot save himself. His prophetic office was mocked when they took a blindfold and put around his eyes, and slapped him with their hands and said, "Prophesy, thou prophet. Tell us who smote you." So all that was precious and sacred to our Lord was ridiculed. They mocked his kingship; they mocked the role of his priest; and they mocked his prophetic office.

Finally, they took him out the lonely way to Golgotha. Have you ever really thought about death by crucifixion? Perhaps a Roman soldier jumped across one of his arms and took a 5" pin and drove it into the tree, then his other arm, then his feet. His hands and feet were pierced according to Psalms 22 and other passages. Then perhaps they raised the cross and let it into the hole that had been prepared and for six agonizing hours our Lord slowly died. He didn't have to die. He said, "You do not take my life away from me, I lay my life down." If Mohammed

Ali came up and began to shove one of us, more than likely we would not shove back. But if some little 4' man came up and started to shove us, more than likely we would shove back. But our Lord did not shove back. "As a lamb dumb before his shearers, so he opened not his mouth." So our Lord could have come down from the cross. He was not held by the force of the nails but by the great love that he had for you and for me. Paul said, "It is this love that sets me on fire for God. It is this love that compels me to serve God."

Then the Lord experienced all that death can offer: No doubt there was dizziness, cramps, thirst, and gangrene began to set in his body. The arteries, especially around the stomach and head, became swollen with surcharged blood. Many who were being so executed would cry out for the executioner to take their life because even death would be a blessed and exquisite release from the agony they were experiencing. Paul said, "It is this cross behind me that keeps me going on."

Brethren, have we read of the cross of our Lord so often that it has lost the force in our life? Is it possible today that we are not the kind of men and women and young people that we should be because we do not have a deep appreciation for the cross of our Lord? I am convinced that those of us, by the eye of faith, will on the way to hell, or heaven, have to go by the foot of the cross of Jesus. I am convinced that those that are lost in the confines of hell will be able to look and see for the first time really the great love that Jesus had for them and the agony that he really experienced from the height of Golgotha, and I am convinced that we will have a deeper and greater appreciation for all that Jesus was willing to do for us. We, too, must glance back at the cross and see what our salvation cost him.

Paul was motivated and Paul said, "I am ready to preach the gospel. (Prothumon euangelisasthai) I have a burning desire to preach the good news of Jesus not only to the wise, but also the unwise; not only to' the elite but also men and women of poverty; not only to those who are highly educated but to those who cannot write their own name nor read." Paul was motivated to preach the gospel of Christ and Paul did not take this as a sideline. He said, "As much as in me is ... " I wonder if this is our attitude. We should all be like Paul. First, we should have a willing ear to hear the Call of Christ from above. Secondly, we should be mindful of the Crowds around us who are dependent upon us for their knowledge of the gospel of Christ. Thirdly, the reward of the promised Crown before us should make us all strive to "fight the good fight." Fourthly, an awareness of the Catastrophe below should motivate us to win souls. Fifthly, we should be moved to preach the gospel because of the Cross behind us.

Paul was a man with a burning heart. Are we?

ENCOURAGING GROWTH IN THE LOCAL CHURCH: LARGE CITY

FREED-HARDEMAN LECTURES
1983

On May 23, 1939, the submarine Squalus, sank off the coast of Portsmouth, New Hampshire. The famed McCann rescue bell was used for the first time. Through this bell-shaped valve, an attempt was made to rescue the 33 men trapped inside. When the rescue squad reached the stricken submarine, they tapped with metal on the hull trying to pinpoint the sailors. The imprisoned men answered in similar fashion. They responded with a question: It was not, "Will I receive hazardous duty pay? It was not "How's the stock market doing?" Their one question was, "Is there any hope?" Sometimes situations become so bad the only thing of importance becomes, "Is there any hope?"

We are living in such times. All across the nation in the cities, the suburbs, and rural communities, there exists crime, drugs, violence, graft, greed, and decline in the behavior of sports heroes, and coaches. The person who holds the highest office in the land has brought the bar of morality and ethics so low that all we can cry is "Is there any hope?"

There is! God promised hope in the sending of his son (Jn. 1:11; Jn 3:16; Ro. 5:8). [All scripture references are taken from the King James Version unless otherwise noted.] Jesus brought that hope when he died on the cross and established the church. That was the hope of the ancient world and is still the hope of the world today. The hope of the world can be found in growing, vibrant congregations committed to taking the Lord's commission seriously—going into the highways, streets, and communities of our nation, cities, suburbs, and rural communities to deliver the "good news," the message of hope.

Attendees are aware that the focus for this hour has been encouraging growth in the local church. The topic for this hour is "encouraging growth in the local church with emphasis on church growth in large cities." In order to have a clearer understanding of the assigned subject definition of terms is essential. The word "encouraging" means the act of inspiring, stimulating, and giving hope (Webster 410).

The word "growth," as used in this context, refers to both the numerical increase and the spiritual development of a congregation. The phrase "local church," refers to the family of God in a given area. The operandi of God in all his redemptive work is through the local church. In fact, everything God has demanded of his people is done through the local congregation. The universal church never functions in the primary work God has assigned his people. It surprises some to learn that the use of the word "church" is limited to only fourteen references to the universal concept, whereas more than one hundred occurrences favor a single or distinct society of Christians.

Essentials for local church growth for the rural, small towns, and large cities are fundamentally the same. After all, it is the same gospel taught to persons with the same problem of sin, and the same Lord who gives the increase. Having noted this, it must be observed that the methodology in these settings will have variations.

Problems Associated with Church Growth

Each local congregation experiences problems brought about by her location. This is especially true in large cities. Why? To answer this question attention must be given to reports by church growth researchers. These researchers have turned to the field of pathology and have adopted eight of the numerous analyzers used by pathologists to explain the causes of decline and death and applied them to the decline and death of churches (Wagner 1-18). These are as follows: (1) ethnikitis caused when the community of old neighborhood church changes ethnically, (2) old age caused by the young leaving and not being replaced, (3) people blindness is a malady often caused by cultural differences between groups in the church field, (4) hyper-cooperativism which is built upon the quality of good will, but it tends to weaken evangelism, not enhance it, (5) koinonitis when the church turns inward to its own fellowship and loves it, (6) sociological strangulation created by a lack of space, whether reference is parking space, worship space, or education space, (7) arrested spiritual development which means that members remain in spiritual infantilism and fail to grasp the mission of the church, and finally (8) St. John's syndrome when a church reaches its goals and begins to ease off.

These analyzers can certainly be applied to the problems in growth experienced by churches in large metropolitan communities. Cities, by their very nature, are places of diversity and shifting neighborhoods. Added to this is the disconnectedness of its people to each other, the neighborhood and the community. All of these intensify the possibility that each of the eight problems described above will occur in an urban church.

The sad truth is that urban churches are not really growing. Some have swollen to a respectable size, but few have grown because members are leading relatives and friends to the Master.

While it is recognized that self-examination is often painful, it is important to be realistic. One has only to look at the general decline in membership of the average congregation, note the failure in church bulletins of reported conversions, and the hoary heads occupying the pews to know that, generally speaking, the church is not growing. There has been a decline in the prayers for the lost, the personal involvement to reach the lost, and in many fine congregations there is no organized program of soul winning. Such practices and rationale result in few conversions. A recent survey taken in one of the finest congregations in the state of Alabama revealed that less than 50% of the congregation believed that sharing the gospel with neighbors, friends, and relatives was important.

The assignment of this lecture is to note how a local congregation in a large city with a metro-population of nearly one million was able to grow from a small group of some 200 to a congregation of more than 800 active members. This group has experienced all the problems listed above, yet was able to work through them—sometimes painfully and often very slowly.

Growth Must Be Desired

In order for an urban church to grow there must be a desire to grow. This simplistic and obvious statement must not be overlooked or underestimated in value. Some really do not have any desire that the church grow. Remarks such as, "I like a small church," "I like things just the way they are," "We are getting too many strange people in the congregation," indicate that some really do not desire to grow. For the church to grow there must not be a nonchalant attitude toward the Parthians, Medes, Elamites, and the dwellers in Mesopotamia. At the core of this desire for growth is the understanding that the church, God's family, is the hope of the world. This understanding should cause members to have a burning desire to share this vital message of hope with their relatives and friends. A by-product of this dream is a growing and dynamic church.

This desire for growth, both spiritually and numerically, must begin in the leadership of the congregation. If the leadership does not desire to grow, and does not understand that the church is the hope of the world, then any desire individual members may have is destined to die. Not only must the leadership have the desire, but they must also insure that each program of the church passes the test of, "How does this effort relate to our assigned mission and goals?"

The minster(s) role is to promote both the spiritual and numerical growth through lessons that are biblical, applicable, and relevant. To rehash lessons from an outline book or give a diet of reruns will not change nor inspire. The pulpit and Bible classes he teaches must be the spark that causes the congregation to hunger and thirst for the Word. It isn't enough to be a scholar of God's word if the minister's lessons do not create this hungering and thirsting. As we are aware, the most learned and sound men can preach to a dying church. The minister must also motivate, train, and exemplify concern for souls. He needs to teach an ongoing class in soul winning and demonstrate sound soul winning methods through his own weekly Bible studies.

Elders must lead the congregation in evangelism through personal involvement and in designing outreach programs.

Successful evangelistic programs include local, stateside, and worldwide efforts. They must make certain that the teaching program is evangelistic in nature. Leaders must be sure that the Bible class teachers know the primary mission of the Lord's church. Classes should plan fellowships that will give opportunity for visitors to be invited and welcomed. Adult and teen classes should be asked to turn in names of prospects and teachers should write letters inviting them to classes. Elders should be willing to participate, finance, and lead the membership to growth.

Promoting Growth in Large Cities

Because the subject for discussion in this lesson is church growth in large cities, the programs described will focus on local evangelism.

Television Programs. A major difference in a smaller community and a large metropolitan area is the difficulty in getting the message to the masses. In smaller communities and rural areas a larger banner or a newspaper ad will inform all. This is simply not the situation in metropolitan localities. For these areas, television is the most effective means of publicly communicating the gospel to the unsaved. A quality program, offered on local stations and cables, will open many doors and get the message to the masses.

Mail-outs. Let the postal employee assist in getting the message of Christ to those who are lost. However, in order to be effective, leaders must be certain that the mail-outs are of high quality and professionally done. This is of major importance because there is only one opportunity to make a first impression.

Bible Correspondence Courses. The use of BBC'S is related to mail-outs, but can differ slightly when combined with the old fashion door to door approach. This approach, while not extremely fruitful, will reach some that no other manner could. It is helpful to take the first BBC lesson, along with a prepaid return envelope, when enrolling people. For those interested in enrolling it is of extreme importance to get their name so a follow-up letter of appreciation can be mailed to every door on which workers knock.

Campaigns. A gospel meeting provides the church the opportunity to knock on thousands of community doors in just a few weeks. This type of campaign can provide an evangelistic opportunity for local members but also involves members from other congregations interested in outreach efforts. Typically the meeting will begin on Sunday; this means that the campaign should begin Saturday morning. Experience has shown that Saturday is the best day for finding folks at home. Materials used by the workers should include: (1) a nice brochure that provides information concerning the length of the meeting, the time, and the topics of each lesson; and (2) an article or tract introducing the recipient to Christ and a return to New Testament Christianity.

All involved in this type of effort are blessed: (1) workers from the visiting and the local congregation are bonded together in love as they work together, (2) the doors knocked on are blessed in that they know a church is interested, and (3) the local church where the campaign is conducted is given an opportunity to work as they provide meals and join in the door-knocking effort. Too many times, members are encouraged to participate in both foreign campaigns and stateside campaigns, but have no opportunity to participate in a local campaign (please do not conduct campaigns in other places and fail to have them at home).

Training Classes. It is imperative that members be constantly trained to know how to teach others. Whatever the method (Jule Miller tapes, Tisdale charts, open Bible study, or one locally developed), members most desirous of practicing evangelism must be given the opportunity to develop and refine their soul-winning skills. Training classes not only meet this need but also provide the needed opportunity for encouragement through weekly reports of successes and failures. It is also important to regularly bring in "experts" who will inform and inspire evangelism.

Friendship Evangelism Classes. This class was found to be a successful program in promoting evangelism in the congregation. The program began with a request for those willing to have 12 to 15 people in their homes one night each week for six weeks. There were enough volunteers to enable every night of the week for six weeks to be used to show a brother's tapes on Friendship Evangelism (two each session). This was climaxed by a Saturday morning gathering of all participants and a renewed determination to reach more people.

Visitation Programs. In order to have a dynamic and growing urban church a number of different types of visitation programs are necessary. Following are programs the congregation has found to be most successful.

Monday night Visitation. The goal of this program is to assure that every visitor to our services who lives in the Birmingham area receives a visit. The Monday night visitation members come for a short devotion at 6:30 and make their visit the same evening. A packet has been designed to thank each visitor for his/her visit and invite him/her back. They are informed of the work of the local congregation and always invited to attend a Bible class. This group represents the prime prospects for home studies. In the event there are too few visitors, members are given the name and address of newcomers to the community.

New Converts Visitation. Members of this special visitation group have the assignment to show new converts the "Now that I'm a Christian" films. A second facet of this program is that each week a different family in the congregation is assigned to visit the new convert. This is a critical component in keeping the new convert faithful in a new environment. It must also be noted that it is necessary to have a brother, truly concerned about souls, to teach the New Convert's class which meets each week. Membership Edification Program (MEP). The edification program is divided into teams. The number in each team is based on the number of members involved. Each Tuesday night two of the teams meet. The meetings, which are held at a different team member's home each month, serve as a time of devotion and fellowship for the team members. A simple meal is brought potluck style. The host is responsible for a short devotion and the team captain assigns the visits to be made and completed before the next Sunday. The edification teams visit shut-ins, older members, hospitals and special members who need a visit to encourage. The purposes of this program are to edify one another, show love and concern for each other, and to get Christianity out of the church building.

Area Ministry Program. One of the key requirements to build a growing church is to keep the faithful, faithful. This is particularly difficult in a large urban congregation where the membership comes from so many different areas. It matters little how big the front door is if those entering are exiting the back door. One solution we have found is a well designed, well-executed area-ministry program. In this program, the membership has been divided into 15 smaller areas based on location. Each area has an area minister who oversees the needs of the members in that area. This program has the following advantages: (1) it provides the elders a better insight into the spiritual condition of the membership; (2) members come to know each other better; (3) members are better assisted in problem times; and (4) it promotes better communication. The area minister has the following duties: he is in charge of the area, and he gives assignments to members who meet each Sunday night following the evening services with their area. He gets cards of absentees, conducts the meetings, assigns the visits or phone calls to be made and follows up to see that they have been made. He reports to the elder who works with him. He aids each member of the area in becoming a devoted Christian, assists in promoting quarterly fellowships, knows every member in his area, and knows when and why they are absence. The area ministry program also provides meals in times of death or hospitalization of members in their area.

In conclusion, let us be reminded there is hope for our world although it may often seem as remote as the fate of the men in a metal coffin off the coast of New Hampshire. In fact, not only was there a remarkable recovery of all 33 men, the Squalus was raised and became the only submarine in WWII to sink an enemy battleship. Just as their hope came from above, our hope is anchored in the wisdom and plans of the one who made us all. Our goal must be to have the same determination, concern, and energy of these ancient rescuers, for our mission is far greater than was theirs.

Works Cited

Kelsey, Hubert P. and Francine A. Roberts. Webster's Ninth New Collegiate Dictionary. Springfield, MA: Merriam-Webster Inc, 1984.

Wagner, Peter C. "Pathology," Church Growth II Notebook. Pasadena, CA: Fuller Theological Seminary, n.d.

THE BIBLE SCHOOL PROGRAM PROMOTES EVANGELISM

FREED-HARDEMAN
LECTURES
1985

The topic for this hour is "The Bible School Program Promotes Evangelism." First one needs to examine the term "Bible School" to understand that it means a period of worship when God's people and visitors are arranged into separate groups with a teacher or teachers and students, or learners, for the purpose of instruction in the Word of God.

This teaching or instruction is to impart knowledge found in both the Old and New Testaments. The teachers may be men or women. How- ever, the women can in no way "teach over" or "usurp authority over" the man (1 Timothy 2:11,12). In other words, women may teach other women or children.

The word "program" refers to the plan, method, or arrangement of instruction in harmony with God's word. The word "promote" means to contribute to the growth, enlargement, and advancements of the cause of Christ. Thus the aim of the Bible school is to promote the knowledge of the word in such a way as to enhance all other efforts of the church. Evangelism is a word derived from the Greek word evangelizo; this word means the fervent, zealous promulgation of the gospel. To recapitulate, the task before us is to give instruction in how Bible classes-Sunday morning, Sunday Evening, mid-week and others-can reach the unsaved through an in-depth study of the Bible. The Bible school finds its authority in our Lord's generic command to teach (Matthew 28: 18-20). The church at Corinth had at least two meetings in which edification was done-one where women could, and did, edify or teach (1 Corinthians 11:5) and one where they could not teach (1 Corinthians 14:34, 35).

During the period when the Roman church held such tight reins on religious activities, little was done in Bible Class arrangements to give instructions to the masses. Making the Bible a "mystery" too deep for the average understanding was a tool employed for various purposes: one very main purpose was that an unenlightened people may be controlled. The Bible schools, as we know them, started as a reaction against rationalism and secularlism, and because common man thirsted for more information about God and His goodness.

In 1780, Robert Raike of Gloucester, England, started a Bible school as an experiment: this experiment was for the purpose of preventing vice. Other Sunday Schools were begun by Raike: and after three years, the results were made public. The success of this effort was so great that at Raike's death 400,000 pupils were enrolled in the English schools.

The Sunday, or Bible School, movement found favor in America because people saw the need for Bible teaching. In 1786 the first Sunday School in the U.S. was organized in the home of William Elliott in Virginia. October 3, 1832, marks the date of the first National Sunday School Convention. Since that time millions have engaged in a common task of teaching the Bible in Bible classes.

Among our brethren, the Sunday school had a belated start. In the early years of the Restoration movement, the movement was promoted almost exclusively by evangelistic preaching.

Campbell, Stone, and other leaders, at first, viewed the Bible classes as "outside institutions." By 1850, the Sunday schools had gained a strong foothold among the more progressive congregations. By 1900, a majority of the congregations had made provisions for at least some very crude Sunday morning Bible study. Gradually the growth of the special classes for study became a part of the services of the church.

During the '60's the church was one of the leading groups in reference to growth. Many factors contributed to this growth, but one of the most important factors was the emphasis given to evangelism in our Bible classes. Many of our people really believed the adage that "as the Sunday school goes, so goes the church." Because they believed this truism, the Sunday study was given much emphasis. Brethren, most of our congregations are experiencing a period of very little, or none at all, growth. Much time has already been spent in this lecture looking historically at the Bible school; history is interesting, but the moment has come to focus on the one major concept important for study.

C. B. Eavey, a former chairman of the Department of Education at Wheaton College, in his study-graph, "History of Christian Education," again and again shows the growth decline factor of Sunday school is in direct correlation with the emphasis given to the Bible. (5) The very purpose of the early denominational organizational Sunday school was to teach the Bible and the Bible only. Whenever this was done (1872-1903), the churches expanded; but when forgotten, churches experienced a decline in growth (1916-1940).

Thus one is made aware of the main reason for the Bible school: Evangelism. For the Bible school to promote evangelism, may I offer the following five suggestions:

1. **There must be an understanding of the purpose of our Bible school.** What is this purpose? First, the students are to have a general knowledge of the Bible and skills to participate in independent study. They should also have enough knowledge to apply these scriptural lessons to every day living. Students should also know that their main purpose in life is to glorify God and this glorification is impossible without concern for the lost.

An understanding of this purpose gives motivation to our efforts. There are at least five motivating factors for evangelism: First, we are evangelistic because we are commanded by our Lord (Mark 16:15). No good soldier can ignore an order from his commander. Second we are evangelistic because of great opportunities around us. Third, we are evangelistic because of the joy of soul winning. An honor is given every Christian, unknown even to the angels, and that honor is the privilege of telling the story of Calvary to those who are lost. Fourth, we are evangelistic because of what it really means to be lost. Fifth, we are evangelistic because of what our salvation cost Christ. Thus we are motivated out of a deep appreciation of what our Lord has done for us.

2. **For our Bible schools to promote evangelism, evangelism must be promoted from the pulpit.** As the pulpit goes, so goes the church. When the pulpit is indifferent and fails to keep before the congregation constantly that its express purpose is to

reach the lost, there can be no hope for evangelism from the Bible classes. The pulpit must not be content with "status quo." The pulpit must not be satisfied with a swelling brought by stealing sheep.

Brother H. A. Dixon often said, "We will never evangelize the world until we believe the world is lost and until we believe we are lost, unless we evangelize."

3. For the Bible school to promote evangelism, the teachers must be evangelistic. The 1922 Abilene Lectureship found James Cox making the statement that of "all the sorry teaching which is found in the world, the sorriest is in the modern Sunday school." He gave as a reason for his statement the following reasons: 1. Poorly prepared and poorly trained teachers; 2. the short period of time devoted to actual teaching; 3. the long interval between classes; 4. the general lack of proper classrooms and equipment; and 5. the general lack of seriousness of purpose.

Every Bible teacher should feel that it is a sin to fail to teach students the importance of evangelism. Yet to be a good teacher, one should be an example of what he teaches. Unless a teacher meets qualifications, there is little need to try to teach. Most large denominations, with growing Sunday schools, expect their teachers to visit the homes of each pupil at least once a year. This visiting provides a wonderful opportunity to influence those family members who are not Christians. Personal interest in each student goes a long way in selling evangelism to the individual.

4. **For the Bible school to promote evangelism, the material taught must be evangelistic.** Our people, for the most part, will do as well as they are taught. How long has it been since the material you are teaching has called attention to the need for being evangelistic? When visitors come to our classes, do they leave with a lesson from God's word, or do they get a "sugar on the slate" moralistic lesson? Maybe we need to put up our coloring books and do away with our "sand piles" and go back to our "card" classes where children came away with God's word hidden in their hearts (Psalms 119:9-11). Unless our Bible lessons are distinctive, we have little need for them. Jesus said that he came "to give the abundant life" (John 10:10). This message must be stressed at all levels until the student really believes it. The basis of our faith is Bible facts, not platitudes. Many platitudes are offered by our religious neighbors; they say "be good because Jesus was good." Now this is a good idea, but faith requires more than philosophy. Yet all teachings are useless unless they are applied to our lives. Facts will not save; a man can go to torment with a Bible under his arm; his head can be full of scriptures and his heart can be full of sin. However, the more Bible facts one knows, the more vivid God's word becomes in his life.

5. **Finally, in order to really promote evangelism through the Bible school, there must be emphasis from the pulpit; dedicated, trained teachers; purposeful plans; and proper goals.** We cannot go where God wants unless we set our goals for that purpose. Without that purpose, teaching becomes a game with no rules, no winners, nor losers. In other words, no game can be won without a goal. Our goals must be spiritually oriented. We can bring in pupils by offering gimmicks; if they come for the

helicopter ride, when the reward is gone, so will go their interest.

In the face of many of the wrong kinds of promotional gimmicks, let us not be guilty of throwing out the baby with the bath water. We can make our studies interesting; we can make our classes enjoyable; we can make our classrooms attractive; but all is lost if we do not have the proper goals. Instead of "like the Indian riding off in all directions" floundering in indecision, all classes must set worthy, realistic goals and diligently work toward attaining them. One concept taught in its entirety is far better than trying to aim at a dozen moving targets at once.

Brethren, we are involved in the greatest of all works; let us not grow weary in doing well. Let us earnestly and prayerfully try to promote evangelism through our Bible school program. This trying may require gigantic efforts and much money spent in realistic teacher training; but, the future of the church lies in the hands of our people. As the prophet once said: "My people are destroyed from a lack of knowledge." Will you take the risk of having destruction laid at your feet? We cannot fail our Bible schools, for in them lie the seeds of and for evangelism.

HOW TO GET
ALONG WITH
OTHERS

Many times we resolve that in some areas we are going to do better. Perhaps one area in which many of us could stand improvement is in the area of trying to get along better with our relatives and with our friends and with our neighbors. Some of us are very difficult to live with and hard to get along with. You have heard, haven't you, of the man whose wife could not please him. Whatever she did was wrong. He was always critical of her. One day she decided she was going to fix him up, so for breakfast he always wanted two eggs. She boiled one of them and fried the other. She served them to him and sure enough, he found something wrong. He said, "You have fried the wrong egg this morning." Some people are very difficult to get along with. Yet the Bible, over and over again, emphasizes the fact that we ought to be able to get along with our fellowman.

Let's mention a couple of these passages.

"If it be possible, as much as lieth in you, live peaceably with all men." (Romans 12:18)

Paul, of course, gave some leeway because there are some people who are against right doing and these people we are not to pacify. But Paul said, "If it be possible, as much as lieth in you..." Go to the very nth degree. "...as much as lieth in you, live peaceably with all men."

"Blessed are the peacemakers: for they shall be called the children of God." (Matthew 5:19)

"Dearly beloved, avenge not yourselves, but rather give place unto wrath: for it is written, Vengeance is mine: I will repay, saith the Lord." (Romans 12:19)

On today's telecast I want to discuss with you some ways and some characteristics that we need to have in our lives that will help us to get along better with others. First, we need to be humble people. We need to have humility in our lives if we are going to get along with others. In Matthew 18, the Lord's disciples were quarreling. Their argument was an argument that, though we may not say publicly, often is in our own heart, "Who is going to be closest to the Lord? Who is going to be the top man?" One wanted to sit on his right hand and the other on the left. The other disciples found out that James and John and their mother, the wife of Zebedee, had made this request and they were quarreling. Jesus brought a young child and sat this young child in the midst of them.

"...Verily I say unto you. Except ye be converted, and become as little children, ye shall not enter into the kingdom of heaven." (Matthew 18:3)

So we need to be humble individuals. In 1 Corinthians 1, the church was having difficulty. There was division among the brethren and they having quarrels. So Paul raised this question, who is Paul, who is Apollos, who is Cephas; we are all men. Some were lining up behind Paul and saying, "I am of Paul." Others were saying, "I am of Apollos" and other's saying, "I am of Cephas." Then Paul said that these were just men.

"Is Christ divided? Was Paul crucified for you? Or were ye baptized in the name of Paul?" (1 Corinthians 1:13)

His argument is that we need to follow the Lord Jesus Christ. Notice Paul's humility.

Paul did not say he was better than Apollos or better than Peter. Paul said who am I that men should follow after me. So in order for us to get along better with other, we are going to have to be individuals with humility.

A second characteristic if we want to get along better with others is that we need to realize our limitations. Have you ever thought about the fact that none of us are masters in every area of life. I know men who are highly educated who can do very little in other fields. I know in my own life personally, though I have been to school practically all of my life and am still a student here in Birmingham and I have enough hours to choke a dog to death; yet the very simplest of things, mechanically speaking, just throw me for a loop. Yet here is a man out here that maybe hasn't even finished high school and he knows how to dismantle a car and put it back together and it will run.

All of us have our limitations and we need to realize this. So often we try to make others come up to the standard we have set for them. Because of this, we find it very difficult to get along with others. In dealing with our children, often we expect them to behave like mature adults. We need to give them time and room to grow up because they are going to make mistakes and we need to be aware of this great principle.

We need to practice the Golden Rule. "Therefore all things whatsoever ye would that men should do to you, do ye even so to them: for this is the law and the prophets." (Matthew 7:12)

So we need to treat others like we want to be treated. If you would get along with your fellowman, there is no improvement on this great rule more than 1900 years old; yet it is as new as the daily newspaper.

"Therefore all things whatsoever ye would that men should do to you, do ye even so to them; for this is the law and the prophets." (Matthew 7:12)

In other words, the whole law of God revolves around this great principle that you treat others as you are desirous of being treated by others. This is a great rule about how to get along with others. There are some important words that somebody has written. Some body said that the six most important words in the English language are these words, "I admit I made a mistake." If you want to get along with others, you need to learn these six words in the English language, "I admit I made a mistake." Yet these are hard for many of us to say and probably for you to say. It is difficult for us to take the blame that we really deserve. We want to pass the buck, we want to blame somebody else. Yet we need to learn the six most important words in the English language, "I admit I made a mistake."

The five most important words are these. We are talking about how to get along with our fellowman, how to get along with our children, how to get along with our companion and how to get along with the people that we work with. Here are the five most important words in the English language according to some, "You do a good job." Often there is a tendency for us to become despondent and discouraged and somebody will come along and say these five important words, "You do a good job." How meaningful this is.

The four most important words in all of the English language are, "What is your opinion?" People like to be asked, we all do, and it brings us in and makes us part of the group. So here are the four most important words, "What is your opinion?"

The three most important words are these, "If you please."

The two most important words, "Thank you." It takes so very little for us to say these two most important words, the words, "Thank you."

The one most important word as far as getting along with others is concerned is the word "we."

The least important word as far as getting along with others is the word "I." So we need to practice the Golden Rule.

We need to treat our fellowman like human beings, which they are, and even if they have characteristics in their lives that we do not particularly admire, we need to realize that, "there but for the grace of God go I." We do not know all of the difficulties that they have encountered in life and these environments of life, to a very great degree, have made them that they are. So we need to learn this principle, "there but for the grace of God go I."

How to get along with others—live a life of humility, realize that all people have their limitations, and thirdly, practice the Golden Rule as taught by our Lord in his discourse in the Sermon the Mount.

HOPE FOR THE HOME

Dad's sermons often do not truly reflect the strength of who he was. Nowhere is this seen as clearly as when he preached on family. He loved mom and each of his children and grandchildren but was rarely sappy or overly emotional about that. He was more formal believing that God's Word should trump evoked emotions. What you, the reader need to know most clearly is that Dad lived the life at home he preached from the pulpit. He was a Christian at home first.

J & D

"Except the Lord build the house they labor in vain that build it..." (Psalm 127:1)

We could well say that except the Lord builds a home, those who are trying to make it a happy home are laboring in vain. When people leave God out of the home, then the home can never be as God would have it to be. There may be those viewing our telecast today who are literally living like they did in the days of the Tower of Babel where there is frustration, confusion and disappointed hope. A happy wedding, a joyous wedding does not make a happy home. Sincere love on the part of the bride and groom will not make, in and of itself, a happy home. Pious mottos scattered throughout the home and expressions of a meaningful nature will not make a happy home.

Today I want to talk to you on the subject , "The Hope of the Home." The Bible says that if the Lord builds the house, then there will be a little bit of heaven upon this earth. The Bible says, God speaking, if you will follow my ways, I will multiply your days; if you will follow my ways, I will multiply the days of your children and if you will follow my ways, your days will be as heaven upon the earth (Deuteronomy 11:21). A home without Christ is divided.

"...Every kingdom divided against itself is brought to desolation; and every city or house divided against itself shall not stand." (Matthew 12:25)

A home in which there is always fussing and bickering and fighting, a husband against the wife, children against parents; certainly that home cannot stand as God would have it to stand. Today there are certain safeguards that the Bible gives us that will make our home the kind of home that God would have it to be.

What is the hope of the home? Number one, the hope of the home, I submit to you, is the old-time family altar. "And these words, which I command thee this day, shall be in thine heart: and thou shalt teach them diligently unto thy children, and Shalt talk of them when thou sittest in thine house, and when thou walkest by the way, and when thou liest down, and when thou risest up. And thou shalt bind them for a sign upon thine hand, and they shall be as frontlets between thine eyes. And thou shalt write them upon the posts of thy house, and on thy gates. (Deuteronomy 6:6-9)

The Bible says that the family altar is the hope of the home today. I one time read about a Chaplain that lived in Arkansas and he said that of the some 17,000 men who had appeared before him in the military, there was only one who was convicted who came from a Christian home and later that conviction was over turned. God said of Abraham, I know him and I know that he will guide his children after him and they will walk in my ways. God realized the importance of the life of Abraham. Abraham had a family altar. Abraham taught his children to fear God. Abraham taught his children the importance of prayer and the importance of following in God's way. Especially is this important today when God has virtually been banned f rom the public school system. How much we need to have the old- time family altar where mother and father will sit around with their children and will read the Bible and will study the Bible with them. Think what an impression this will make, what an impression for good upon America if the people would return to simple Bible study in the home and pray together as members of God's family.

In the second place, the hope of the home is the old-time family pew. Not only do we need to have God in our home, not only do we need to read his word and to pray to him daily in our lives and work for him; we also need to worship him. "Not forsaking the assembling of ourselves together, as the manner of some is; but exhorting one another: and so much the more, as ye see the day approaching." (Hebrews 10:25) Do you attend the Bible study? Do you attend worship? I wonder how many thousands of people there may be viewing our telecast today that never darken the doors of any meeting house any where. There are three reasons why ever y family needs to be in services every Sunday. Number one, because that is what God wants us to do. That is what the Lord Jesus wants us to do. There are those that say, "Preacher, if you can show me in the Bible in black and white where God wants me to worship him, then I will be there."

"But seek ye first the kingdom of God, and his righteousness; and all these things shall be added unto you." (Matthew 6:33)

Are you seeking the kingdom of God first in your life when you abandon that which God allowed Jesus to give his life to establish? Jesus loved the church. He calls us his bride. He calls it his body. You would not do violence to the physical body of the Lord were he on the earth. What about the spiritual body— the church of the Lord? What about harming the bride of Christ? You say you just didn't realize the church was that—but that is what the Bible refers the church to—the bride, the body of Christ, as the family of God and when you ridicule the importance of the church, you are ridiculing the very family of God. We need to realize when we do not attend the services and worship God, we are voting to close the doors of the meeting house, I am leaving God out of my life, I am not giving my children the kind of training they need.

Judge Sam Tatum, a juvenile judge in the courts of Nashville, Tennessee, in days gone by, had thousands and thousands of young teenage boys and girls stand before him for sentencing. He made this remarkable assertion, 'in all the days that I have been practicing law, I have never had to sentence a young man or a young woman to reform school whose parents, along with them, attended a Sunday school.' So we need to be in Sunday school and we need to be worshipping God. Reason number one is because that is what the Lord wants us to do.

Reason number two is because of the matter of influence." Let your light so shine before men, that they may see your good works and glorify your Father which is in heaven." (Matthew 5:16) When I fail to worship, then I am not letting my light shine. I am not giving God the glory and honor he so longs for and so deserves.

In the third place, I need to be present with my family because when I am present, it is for my own benefit. Many of us are filled with such pride and egotism that we stroll into the meeting house some Sunday as though God owes us a big debt and we take the attitude that God should feel fortunate to have someone as fine as I am. Really worship will not benefit God. Worship is for our own benefit.

You recall back in grammar school when you were caught talking when you should not talk and the teacher told you to write a thousand times, "I will not talk in class." You remember how you used to get two or three pencils and write on a line to expedite the matter. You brought that to the teacher. That really didn't help the teacher. The teacher gave that assignment for your benefit. So I am suggesting to you that worship is for our benefit. It fortifies us against the problems and temptations of life. The hope of America, the hope of our world, the hope of the home—number one is the old-time family altar where we meet around and study the word of God together, where we pray as families . That old song, "If I Could Only Hear My Mother Pray Again" is a laughing stock in many circles today because young people have never heard their parents pray. Then second, we need to return to the family pew where mother and father, son and daughter make their way each Sunday to the meeting house and pour out their heart of praise and adoration to God. There are three reasons why we need to worship. Because that is what Jesus wants; because worship will show that we are giving glory and honor to God; because worship, after all, is for our own personal benefit.

We are living in a time today, more than anytime ever in the history of our country, when we need to return to the old-time family altar and the family pew. What about your home? Is it the kind of home God would have it to be? Are you failing in the home? You may be a successful business man, you may be a successful woman in the business realm; but, my friends, if our homes are not what they should be, then in the eyes of God we are failing. What about your home? The hope of the home—the old-time family altar and the family pew.

I HAVE SINNED

One of my favorite cartoon characters is Dennis the Menace, in one cartoon of Dennis he is depicted sitting under a large picture window which has a hole in it. Dennis has a sling-shot in his hand. His father is asking Dennis how the window was broken, Dennis replies," I was cleaning my sling-shot and it went off." Many of us are like Dennis we endeavor to excuse our misconduct.

This attitude is shown to be very true as one notices how infrequently the expression "I have sinned" occurs in the Bible. Of the thousands of Bible characters whose lives are described in the word of God fewer than 20 said, "I have sinned."

For the next two Sundays we will examine four times this expression occurs and discuss some lesson from them.

One would think the expression "I have sinned" would have first fallen from the lips of Adam and Eve when they violated Gods laws in the Garden of Eden, but as we search the early chapters of God's book we find no such admission.

One would certainly think after Cain slew his brother his conscience would have caused him to freely confess his sins, but as we search through the Bible account of his actions we find no such statement.

Many times we are surprised at the admissions of men who live very wicked lives. The confession "I have sinned" first fell from the lips not of a very Godly and pious individual, but a man who had no respect or regard for God. The expression first occurs in Exodus 9:27, as the various plagues where brought against Pharaoh and the Egyptians, concession began to be offered. When one reads of the 7th plague he notes for the first time the fear Pharaoh has. In the midst of this fear Pharaoh said, "I have sinned."

When the lightening had ceased to brighten the heavens and the thunder subsided Pharaoh was again hardened and since his fear was gone the humility evidenced in his confession was also gone.

When people today confess sin in times of fear. As an uncle of mine in a fox hole in World War II penned a letter which I read in which he promised if God would let him get out of the war alive he would make the Lord a faithful servant. The war has long since ended, but when the fear of battle was no longer in his heart he forgot his promise and has seldom darkened the door of the church building.

What about you? When you were involved in an accident, from a hospital bed, or were fearful for the life of a loved one were you as Pharaoh willing to change your life?

A second time the expression "I have sinned" occurs in the Bible is in Joshua 7 after Israel had defeated Jericho a man violated Gods specific instructions that they were to salvage nothing of the ruins. Achan violated this law and when Isarel went against Ai, they were severely embarrassed and more than 30 men were killed.

Joshua in sack cloth and ashes ask God for explanation of their defeat it was then that God Informed Joshua of sin in the camp. After examination of the various tribes and families it was discovered that Achan had the spoils and he admitted, "I have sinned."

The lesson here is that "no man is an island to himself." They took Achan and killed him, but this is not all. They also killed his wife and his children. When we sin it affects the lives of others.

The third time the expression "I have sinned" occurs falls from the lips of the only man in all of the Bible to be called, "a man after Gods own heart." On one occasion, David was idle. He saw a beautiful woman by the name of Bathsheba. He lusted for her and committed adultery with her, then to cover his ungodly deed he sent her husband to the front lines with his own death warrant. When Nathan, the prophet of God, confronted him with his deed, David said, "I have sinned."

In Psalm 51:12-13, David said, if God would forgive him he would "teach transgressors" and "convert sinners." The lesson here is that the natural feeling to forgiveness and the grace of God is a feeling of obligation toward our fellowman.

The fourth time we notice this expression occurring in the Bible is in the life of the Prodigal Son, I am sure all of our viewers are familiar with the details of how he left home and wasted his money in sin. In the hog pen he decided to return home. This he did and confessed to his father "I have sinned" against heaven and earth. The great lesson here is the attitude that God has toward those who in the right spirit are willing to confess their sins. Isn't it wonderful that we serve a God who is willing to forgive if we will but accept forgiveness on his terms?

I HAVE SINNED

✓ PHARAOH - Ex. 9:27 (1)
            Ex. 10:16 (2).

Balaam   num. 22:34 (3)

Achan - Josh. 7:20 (4)

Saul.   1 Sam. 15:24 (5)
        1 Sam. 15:30 (6)
        1 Sam. 26:21 (7)

David - 2 Sam. 12:13 (8) ✓
              19:20 (9) ✓
Psm. 41:4 (16) ✓   24:10 - (10) ✓
   51:4 - (17) ✓   24:17 (11) ✓
              1 Chronicles 21:8 (12) ✓
              1 Ch. 21:17 (13) ✓
   Nehemiah   neh. 1:6 (14)

Job. Job. 7:20 (15)

Micah. micah 7:9 (18)

Judas☩ matt 27:4 (19)

Prodigal Son Lk 15:8 (20)
_____
9 People + Prodigal   David - 8 Times
Total of 20 times

We Have sinned

Num. 12:11
Num. 14:40
Num. 21:7
Deut 1:41
Josh 10:10
Josh 10:15

1 Sam. 7:6
1 Sam 12:10
1 Kings 8:47
2 Chron. 6:37
Neh. 1:6
Psa 106:6
Jer. 64:5
Jer. 3:25
Jer. 8:14
Jer. 14:7
Jer. 14:20
Lam. 5:16
Dan 9:5
Dan 9:8
Dan 9:15

Total of 21 times —

Ye have sinned

Ex. 32:30
  32:31 - thir people have sinned

num. 32:23

Deut 9:16 - ye had sinned -
Deut 9:18 - ye sinned
Josh 7:11 Israel hath sinned
1 Sam. 14:33 - People sinned
1 Kings 8:33 - They have sinned
1 Kings 8:35 They have sinned
1 Kings 8:50 people that have sinned
1 Kings 14:16 Jeroboam sinned
1 Kings 15:30 Jeroboam sinned
1 Kings 16:13 - they sinned
1 Kings 16:19 - he sinned
2 Kings 17:7 - Israel hath sinned
2 Kings 21:17 - he sinned
2 chr. 6:24 they
2 chr. 6:26 they
2 chr. 6:37 people
neh. 1:6 my father's house
neh 9:29 people
neh 13:26 solomon.

Job 1:5 - my sons
. Psa. 78:32 - they
. Jer. 43:27 - fathers sinned
. Jer. 33:8 - they
. Jer. 33:8 they
. Jer. 40:3 - ye
. Jer. 44:23 ye
. Jer. 50:7 - They
. Jer. 50:14 - she
. Lam. 1:8 - Jerusalem
. 5:7 - Our fathers
. Ezek 28:16 - he
. 28:16 Thou
. 37:23 - They
. Hos 4:7 - They
. 10:9 - Thou
. 13:2 - They
. Hab 2:10 - hast (Israel) sinned
. Zeph 1:17 - They

Total of 41 times

BARNABAS

Many of the Jews had come to the city of Jerusalem for the purpose of keeping the Feast of Pentecost and when they heard about the fact that they had taken Jesus and they had crucified Him and that he had been raised from the dead, many of them believed the gospel that was proclaimed and so they didn't want to go back home; they enjoyed this fellowship, this love that they had one for another. This brought about a need because these Christians, these who had been converted to Christianity, had to have some way to live; they needed a shelter and food. The Bible says that these early Christians sold their possessions and they brought the money and laid it at the feet of the apostles and distribution was made as every man had need.

In Acts, chapter 4, we read of one of these disciples. The Bible says in verse 36, "And Joses, who by the apostles was surnamed Barnabas, (which is being interpreted, The son of consolation,) a Levite, and of the country of Cyprus, having land sold it and brought the money, and laid it at the apostles' feet." There are a number of observations that I want to make, to begin with the apostles called Joses by the name Barnabas. I have often wondered what the apostles would call us. I wonder if he wouldn't call some in the congregation Gossip; if the apostles wouldn't name some of them Strivers, or those who created strife within the congregation. I am sure he would term some people Happy, but they called this particular disciple of the Lord by the name of Barnabas which means "son of consolation" or "son of exhortation."

He was exuberant, he tried to get people to do the will of God. This man is one of the most generous men of all the Bible. You know when you think about outstanding Bible characters there is usually some predominant trait in their life. For example, if I told you about a man who had great faith more than likely you would think about this great servant of God by the name of Abraham. If we were talking about those men who have patience, more than likely you would think about a man like Job who had patience and who so patiently endured the afflictions and the sufferings brought about by old Satan. But this particular man was known by the name of Barnabas and he is known as a very generous man. I want to make three observations about his life.

First of all, he had a generous hand. He had some land over on the Island of Cyprus and he sold that land and brought the money and laid it at the apostles' feet. He was a Levite; he was a man who had given his all in the service of God. He was a man who looked after the temple or later the synagogue—he was constantly involved in the Lord's work. I wonder today if I am speaking to those of us who are generous, who have generous hands; generous with our time and with our talent, and even with our money.

You know there are people when you begin to talk about money that talk about the widow's mite. In Mark, chapter 12, the Lord's disciples, along with the Lord, were watching as various people came and cast into the treasury of the synagogue. There came in men in all their pompous array and they gave out of their abundance, but there was a lady, a widow who came and cast in only two mites. And every once in a while when a preacher begins to talk about money there are those who say, well I can't do anything but give the "widow's mite." I am reminded of the story of a very wealthy man, a millionaire, and he came to the preacher and he said, "Preacher, here is a check for $10,000.00," he said, "I am going to give the widow's mite." The preacher said, "You owe this church $500,000.00, we'll just accept half of the widow's mite, you owe the church $500,000.00." The millionaire took the check and tore it up, and wrote out another check, this time for $5,000.00, and said, "There you are smart aleck, that cost you $5,000.00." Well, you see this man was using the widow's mite like a lot of us do. The Bible tells us that the widow gave all she had, but if this millionaire had given only half the widow's mite, he would have given $500,000. Let us never be guilty of saying I will give the widow's mite when we cast in our $1.00, or $5.00, unless we have given everything.

You know the Lord isn't really interested in the amount that we are giving; he is interested in what that amount represents— what percentage of our income and our money does this amount that I give really represent. A man shouldn't be embarrassed to put a quarter in the collection plate or fifty cents in the collection plate if he is giving liberally, if he is giving freely, cheerfully and out of love; he shouldn't be embarrassed. This widow evidently wasn't embarrassed and the Lord paid her a supreme compliment, "She has given all that she has." Well the Lord doesn't expect us to give all that we have, but the Lord does expect us to make ,it possible for His work to go on and He expects us to give in order that this work can be carried on.

You know this man Barnabas is the only disciple that is specifically mentioned of the scores and perhaps even hundreds, and possibly even thousands of Christians who were selling

234 - THE LIVING WORD

their possessions and bringing their money and laying at the apostles' feet, there is only one man that they have specifically mentioned by name and that is this man, Barnabas. He was generous in hand.

In the second place, I want to suggest to you that Barnabas was generous in his judgment; he was generous in his judgment. Turn with a few pages over in the Bible this time to the ninth chapter of the Book of Acts and refresh your memory about the fact that there was a man by the name of Saul of Tarsus who was breathing out threatenings and slaughterings against the Church; he was binding Christians, bringing them back to the City of Jerusalem where they were being fed to hungry lions and hungry dogs, and where they were being burned at the stake. For example, he held the garments as they stoned Stephen to death; he consented to the death of Stephen.

Well, this man, of course the Lord appeared to him and told him to go into the city of Damascus and there it would be told him what he must do and a disciple of the Lord named Ananias came to him and found him to be a believer who was a repentant believer, and told him "Now why tarriest thou, arise, and be baptized, and wash away thy sins calling on the name of the Lord." Later Saul of Tarsus said I was not disobedient to the heavenly vision. He carried out the will of God. You can imagine the attitude the early Christian had toward Saul of Tarsus—they were scared to death of him. Here was a man that had been persecuting the church, binding both men and women, hauling them back to the City of Jerusalem and persecuting them in unspeakable ways, and now suddenly he has done an about face. The Bible says here in Acts 9:26, "And when Saul was come to

Jerusalem, he assayed to join himself to the disciples: but they were all afraid of him, and believed not that he was a disciple." They thought why we've got a spy on our hands; he's going to come in and have fellowship with us, but them he'll betray us— but not Barnabas. This man Barnabas was generous in his judgment and the Bible says, "But Barnabas took him, and brought him to the apostles, and declared unto them how he had seen the Lord in the way, and that he had spoken to him, and how he had preached boldly at Damascus in the name of Jesus. "

In the third place, Barnabas was generous in heart—he was generous in heart. In the fifteenth chapter of Acts we read of Paul and Barnabas deciding to go back and re-visit these congregations that they had established. And the Bible says that Barnabas wanted to take with them a young man by the name of John Mark, but Paul didn't want to take John Mark. Why? Well, because John Mark for some reason had returned early on the first missionary journey—maybe he had gotten homesick, maybe he was prejudice against the Gentiles, as Ramsey said, he might have developed malaria fever, but for some reason he wanted to go back home, and Paul said, we are not going to take him on the second missionary journey. But this man, Barnabas, with this generous heart of his, had forgiven John Mark, and he said, let's carry him. The Bible said that the dispute became so great that Barnabas finally said to Paul, you go your way and you take with you Silas, and I'll go my way and I'll take with me John Mark. Later on Paul had to admit that Barnabas was right, for in 2 Timothy, chapter 4, Paul in the last letter he was ever to write said to Timothy, "Bring with you the cloak for it is cold in the winter time and bring with you the parchments and the writings, and he said,"bring John Mark because he is good for me in the mission." And so Barnabas was correct.

When we think of Barnabas, like when we think of Abraham a man of faith, or Job a man of patience, let us think perhaps of this lesser known character of God's Word as a very generous man. Generous in his hand—freely giving to others, generous in his judgment, and generous in his heart. In deed he was a great man.

FOR WHOM IS BAPTISM?

For years every week Dad would record five fifteen minute radio broadcasts for Radio Belize. Dad and mom first went to British Honduras (present Belize) in 19??. The church at Woodlawn had made the decision to consolidate their mission work to one area they would work. At that time BH was the only English speaking country in the world where there was not a church of our Lord's. So for 40 years Dad would go for one week or two twice a year and work in that country. They established congregations in every major city in Belize and many of these are still very healthy churches.

I (Dale) remember one Saturday that Dad was recording the programs and I had stopped by his office to see him. I had not been preaching long. He said: "I take on responsibilities that force me to study."

The sermon that follows is one of the manuscripts of one of the Belize sermons. And, it is also an excellent sermon on baptism.

J & D

Practically everybody that believes that Jesus Christ came and lived among men and gave his life a ransom many, many centuries ago believes in baptism in some manner or another. There are those who christen little babies. There are those who pour water upon one's head. There are those who believe in three baptisms; the first time in the name of the Father, the second time in the name of the Son, and the third time in the name of the Holy Ghost. On today's radio broadcast, we want to look at this important theme and in particular, we study with you today For Whom Is Baptism? We hope you will stay tuned.

Our question on the radio broadcast today: for whom is baptism? If you have a pencil and paper, we invite you to make notation of the things that are going to be said on the radio broadcast today and study them more thoroughly in the privacy of your own home. I just simply want to turn to the Bible and to give book, chapter and verse for the question: for whom is baptism today?

Number one, baptism is for those who are unsaved.

"And he said unto them, Go ye into all the world, and preach the gospel to every creature. He that believeth and is baptized shall be saved; but he that believeth not shall be damned." (Mark 16:15-16)

Those who indicate that one must be saved before he can be baptized finds that he is out of harmony with this particular verse, for those who were to be baptized were those who were unsaved.

In the second place, baptism is for those who have heard. "And Crispus, the chief ruler of the synagogue, believed on the Lord with all his house; and many of the Corinthians hearing believed, and were baptized." (Acts 18:8)

In the third place, baptism is for those who have been taught. "Go ye therefore, and make disciple so fall nations, baptizing them in the name of the Father, and of the Son, and of the Holy Ghost; teaching them to observe all things whatsoever I have commanded you: and, lo, I am with you alway, even unto the end of the world." (Matthew 28:19-20) The King James translation says, "Go ye therefore, and teach all nations, baptizing them in the name of the Father, and of the Son, and of the Holy Ghost: teaching them to observe all things whatsoever I have commanded you: and, lo, I am with you alway, even unto the end of the world." So baptism is for those who have been taught. There is no example in all the Bible of anyone who was ever baptized until first they were taught. Remember, ladies and gentle men, we are just simply accepting what the Bible says on this all important subject, For Whom Is Baptism.

Number four, baptism is for those who receive the word of God.

"Then they that gladly received his word were baptized: and the same day there were added unto them about three thousand souls." (Acts 2:41) So one must be able to receive the word of God before he is a proper subject for Bible baptism.

Number five, baptism is for believers. "He that believeth and is baptized shall be saved; but he that believeth not shall be damned." (Mark 16:16)

"...and the eunuch said. See, here is water; what doth hinder me to be baptized? And Philip said. If thou believest with all thine heart, thou mayest. And he answered and said, I believe that Jesus Christ is the Son of God. And he commanded the chariot to stand still and they went down both into the water, both Philip and the eunuch; and he baptized him." (Acts 8:36-38)

Number six, baptism is for the penitent one. "Then Peter said unto them. Repent, and be baptized every one of you in the name of Jesus Christ for the remission of sins, and ye shall receive the gift of the Holy Ghost." (Acts 2:38)

So baptism is for someone who first repents of their sins. There is not the order of baptism and then repentance, baptism without repentance; but baptism is for those who repent of their wrongs. Acts 2:38, "Repent and be baptized..." Never any reversal of this order. Never any change of this and we would expect Peter to preach and teach the same thing every time he taught on the subject of baptism. We would not believe that the Apostle Peter would preach one thing one day and the next day he would change the message. So Peter says that baptism is for those who have repented of their wrongs. Then baptism is for men and women.

"But when they believed Philip preaching the things concerning the kingdom of God, and the name of the Jesus Christ, they were baptized, both men and women." (Acts 8:12)

Now, ladies and gentlemen, we have noted some seven different groups of people in answer to the question: for whom is baptism. Number one, baptism is for those who are unsaved. Number two, baptism is for those who have heard. Number three, baptism is for those who have been taught. Number four, baptism is for those who have received the word. Number five, baptism is for those who believe. Number six, baptism is for those who have repented of their wrongs. Number seven, baptism is for men and women. This is what the Bible answer is to the question: for whom is baptism.

Now, of course, the Bible teaches the importance of baptism and the necessity of baptism. Baptism is mentioned 100 different times upon the sacred pages of God's Divine Word. There are those who say they don't believe in baptism. If the Bible never mentioned baptism, then such a position would be correct. But the truth of the matter is that baptism is mentioned at least 100 times upon the pages of God's Word. Since it is a Bible subject, it behooves us, therefore, to find out just exactly what is the nature of the commandment regarding baptism. We find that baptism is a burial in water. (Romans 6:4, Colossians 2:12). Baptism is in order to put one into Christ.

"For ye are all the children of God by faith in Christ Jesus. For as many of you as have been baptized into Christ have put on Christ." (Galatians 3:26-27)

Who have been baptized into Christ? "As many of you, " Paul says, "as have been baptized into Christ have put on Christ." I have a coat on today up here in Alabama. It is somewhat cool — not very cool — not below freezing, but I have a coat on. I suppose that at this season of the year there are many of you in the country of Belize who wear sweaters and you put that on. The Bible says that we put on the Lord Jesus Christ. Galatians 3:27, "For as many of you as have been baptized into Christ have put on Christ." Remember, my friends, we are going to be judged on the basis not of what man says, not on the basis of what the preacher says, but we are going to be judged on the basis of what the word of God says.

"He that rejecteth me, and receiveth not my words, hath one that judgeth him:the word that I have spoken, the same shall judge him in the last day." (John 12:48)

If you would like a free copy of the passages that we have presented today on the radio broadcast, if you will write: P. O. Box 526, Belize City, we will be happy to send you a list of these passages in answer to the question; for whom is baptism?

WOMEN
PREACHERS

Have you ever wondered why that in the Bible one never reads that as a results of some good sister preaching thousands ever led to Christ. On tonight's telecast we want to study the question: Do women have a right to preach publicly? It has been well said that God crowned his glorious creation when he caused a deep sleep to come upon Adam and created woman. There are primarily two Bible passages which relate particularly to this study.

The first is recorded in 1 Corinthians 14:34-35. This passage affirms that women are to keep silent in the church. Who are the women being described? From verse 35 it is obvious that they were married women. Here are some women to which this verse would not apply.

1. Unmarried teenage girls
2. Spinsters
3. Widows
4. Woman with a non-christian husband
5. Women with Christian husband who are novices.
6. Women who have husbands who have net grown spiritually as a result of their failure to study and understand the scriptures.

Paul says let your women keep silent. Some have said that this passage refers to the business meetings of the church and that at such gatherings women are to be quiet. This could not be correct because the assembly under discussion was attended by unbelievers (verse 23). By study of the earlier verses in this context He was speaking to the prophets or preachers, (who would interrupt a preacher in a public meeting but his wife?)

Paul is saying that the prophets are not to be interrupted by their wives as they teach God's word.

Those who believe that women have a right to preach probably advocate this being the following reasons:

Women first told of the risen Savior (Matthew 28:8) There is a tremendous difference in women in private conversation telling someone the good news about Christ and standing publicly and preaching His word.

It is also sometimes stated that Phillip had four daughters who prophesied and on the Day of Pentecost it was predicated that the young women would prophesy. The word prophesy means to teach. It is true that the passage indicates that women would teach, but it does not tell us who they would teach. As we will notice later women have a right to teach certain people.

The other passage related to our study is I Tim 2:11-12. According to this passage women are not permitted to teach nor usurp authority. In this passage there are two infinitive phrases modified by a prepositional phrase. Women are to teach:

A. Other women - Titus 2
B. Their own children
C. Men in private as Priscilla had a part in teaching Apollos (Acts 18) But this verse emphatically affirms that they are not to teach over the man. This is precisely what women preachers do. There are many wonderful things that women can do for the Lord, but preaching is not one of them.

IS ONE CHURCH
GOOD AS
ANOTHER?

What is the fastest growing religious group in the world today? I know that last year our Mormon friends spent $550,000,000 on world evangelism. There are many groups that are evidencing a real concern for reaching out to others. I am convinced that in America the fastest growing movement is the nondenominational group. I want to talk about this factor: is one church just as good as another church, and about being nondenominational. Please study with us.

Nondenominational Christianity. They are springing up everywhere, I see them all across the country as I travel. Those who worship in this church building belong to a nondenominational group. Why is it so popular? Perhaps because of the ritualism, the hypocrisy and the formalism that has crept into organized religion, I have often thought about the question: if Jesus were upon the earth today, just where would Jesus worship. I know there are some things that did not impress our Lord. For example, our Lord was not impressed with the showmanship that so often characterizes religion today. He said: Matthew 6:2, "Therefore when thou doest [thine] alms, do not sound a trumpet before thee, as the hypocrites do in the synagogues and in the streets, that they may have glory of men. Verily I say unto you. They have their reward." Matthew 6:5, "And when thou prayest, thou shalt not be as the hypocrites [are]: for they love to pray standing in the synagogues and in the corners of the streets, that they may be seen of men. Verily I say unto you. They have their reward." Matthew 6:16, "Moreover when ye fast, be not, as the hypocrites, of a sad countenance: for they disfigure their faces, that they may appear unto men to fast. Verily I say unto you. They have their reward. Jesus was not impressed with showmanship. Jesus was not impressed with large numbers. The Bible says that great crowds followed Him (John 6). They came from miles and miles away. Thousands of people were adhering to the teaching that He was giving. Some were following because of the loaves and fishes and on one occasion Jesus began to come down hard on some of the things they believed in. The Bible says that many turned and walked no more with Him. Jesus was not impressed with big numbers. Jesus was not impressed with big church buildings, in Mark chapter twelve, a widow cast in only two mites and the disciples asked Jesus: "Have you seen our big fine church building?"

Mark 13:2, "And Jesus answering said unto him, Seest thou these great buildings? there shall not be left one stone upon another, that shall not be thrown down"

Where would Jesus worship were He alive today? Our Lord was impressed - He was impressed with religious honesty. He said the sacrifices of God are a broken spirit.

Psalms 51:17, "The sacrifices of God [are] a broken spirit: a broken and a contrite heart, O God, thou wilt not despise."

Today we want to notice an explanation of nondenominationalism. The word "denomination" simply means, according to The World Book Encyclopedia: "A religious group or a sect, it is a sect with a specific doctrine. It often has a certain name and frequently there is some kind of centralized organization, it is a part of a whole."

When we talk about nondenominational Christianity, one of the things in which we are interested: Was there ever a time when denominationalism did not exist? I am happy to say that there was, indeed, such a time. Paul said to the church at Ephesus: Ephesians 4:4-6, "[There is] one body, and one Spirit, even as ye are called in one hope of your calling; One Lord, one faith, one baptism. One God and Father of all, who [is] above all, and through all, and in you all."

Ephesians 1:22-23, "And hath put all [things] under his feet, and gave him [to be] the head over all [things] to the church. Which is his body, the fulness of him that filleth all in all."

Acts 2:47, "Praising God, and having favour with all the people. And the Lord added to the church daily such as should be saved."

When the church had its beginning, there were not a multiplicity of denominations. There was only one church referred to as the one body of Jesus Christ. One body and that body is the church, and the Lord added all the saved to the church. Somebody might respond by saying: "What about at Corinth, weren't there different churches at Corinth? The household of Chloe brought back the report some said they were following Paul or Cephas or Apollos and some said they were following Christ." May I remind you that all of this was condemned. Paul said: 1 Corinthians 1:10, "Now I beseech you, brethren, by the name of our Lord Jesus Christ that ye all speak the same thing, and [that] there be no divisions among you; but [that] ye be perfectly joined together in the same mind and in the same judgment." Let there be no denominationalism among you is what the Apostle Paul advocated.

Secondly, let's look at the defense of nondenominational Christianity. Some affirm that nondenominational Christianity is impossible because God has left us no pattern. My friends, the Bible does show us a pattern. Galatians 1:6, "I marvel that ye are so soon removed from him that called you into the grace of Christ unto another gospel:" Paul said there was a pattern. Paul said to the Corinthians that he preached the same thing everywhere.

John 16:13, "Howbeit when he, the Spirit of truth, is come, he will guide you into all truth: for he shall not speak of himself; but whatsoever he shall hear. [that] shall he speak: and he will shew you things to come."

There is a pattern and those who advocate there is no pattern are simply ill-informed about the fact that the Bible does advocate there is a pattern. Isn't it strange that some say there is a pattern for morality—that we are to notice the sanctity of marriage—that we are to advocate there is to be no adultery and fornication and no drunkenness by the children of God. They can see that there is a pattern where moral principles are concerned but some say no pattern where the church is concerned. Some say there is no single pattern and when you talk about restoring the church of the Bible and they say, "Which church? The church at Antioch, the church at Ephesus, the church at Corinth?" The similarity of these different churches came from two sources. Some were different in matters of expediency—in matters of judgment, and in matters of judgment we should not bind our opinions upon others. Some, however, failed to heed the apostles' doctrine and they lost their candlestick the book of Revelation says. Jesus cast them out. No longer were they to be His flock.

Others will admit that there is a pattern but it is unnecessary to have nondenominational Christianity because we all belong to the same vine and there are just different branches. We are all headed for the same place. This branch is this church and that branch is another. Jesus said: John 15:5, "I am the vine, ye [are] the branches: He that abideth in me, and I in him, the same bringeth forth much fruit: for without me ye can do nothing. If a man abide not In me, he is cast forth as a branch, and is withered; and men gather them, and cast [them] Into the fire, and they are burned."

He is not talking about various churches—He is not talking about different religious institutions, He is talking about individuals. He said, I am the vine and each individual member of the church is the branch and if the branch does not bear fruit —if that Christian is not productive, he is going to be cut off and cast into the fire. Think about vines. On one vine you do not find oranges growing, apricots growing, watermelons growing. If it is a grape vine, you find all grapes; if it is a watermelon vine, you find all watermelons growing on that vine. My friends, Jesus does not sanction the different religious organizations and denominations and say they all belong to the same vine.

Others object that it is impractical and that if one tries to go back and form a nondenominational group, we are starting another denomination. In response to that I would raise this simple question: What about the church of the first century. If we knew what those people did in New Testament times, wouldn't we be simple Christians? If it takes more than the Bible to be what you are religiously, isn't that being involved too much? Isn't that bringing into religion the teaching of men too much? In that ancient world, people believed in Jesus; they repented of their sins, which simply meant to change their mind about the sinning business; they acknowledged that they believed Jesus to be the Son of God; they were immersed in the name of the Father, Son and Holy Ghost for the remission of sins; and the Lord added them to the church.

Let's suppose that there is a great union meeting. Let's suppose that at this great union meeting we all study the Bible. Two-hundred are present at this union meeting. After we study the Bible and have concluded our Bible Study and after we have done what the Bible tells us to do to become a Christian, fifty of them say: we want to form denomination A. Fifty more say they want to form denomination B. Fifty more say they would like to form denomination C. Suppose fifty of this 200 say they don't want to be any denomination, they want to simply follow what the Bible says—they just want to be Christians. Would that be possible? Indeed, it would be possible.

Today I am defending nondenominational Christianity—to go back to the Bible—to do Bible things in Bible says, do Bible actions in Bible ways and call Bible things by Bible names—to go back to that original pattern.

Thirdly today I make an appeal to you for nondenominational Christianity. If one church is just as good as another church, that could be said about denominations that were built by men. But if one simply follows the Bible, like the fifty who said they just said they wanted to be Christians and worship as the people did in Bible days and have the same goals and aspirations that they did and wear the same name they wore, we form a church. The Lord adds us to that church and we are a member of a nondenominational group.

Is one body as good as another body? You wouldn't advocate that, is your friend's body just as important to you as your own personal body? One body is not as good as another. One spiritual body, the church, is not as good as another, is one bride as good as another bride? Would you advocate that today that it really doesn't matter—after all, one bride is just as good as another bride? The church is called the bride of Jesus Christ, if one church is just as good as another church, then you are saying that one bride is just as good as another bride, if one family as good as another family? The church is the family of God. If you advocate that one church is as good as another, you are advocating that one family is just as good as another family.

Yes, nondenominational groups are popping up all over our land, I am advocating that you belong to a nondenominational group by believing with Jesus with all your heart; by repenting of your sins; confessing that you believe Jesus to be the Son of God; by being baptized according to the teaching of the Bible; and allow God to add you to His church, it is not wrong to change churches if you go back and follow the church of the Bible.

FORGIVENESS

I would be remiss if I did not say a word about that marvelous lunch we had. Just tremendous food and everything I had was just delicious. Thank you very much for all of the work and the effort that you put forth. It has been a real delightful day. It is unusual to preach right after lunch, it is hard enough to keep folks awake during the regular Sunday afternoon or evening service. I do remember some experiences about folks that went to sleep. I was preaching in Hamilton, AL and our song leader went to sleep. So I shouted a couple of time hoping to wake him up but that didn't do any good so I got down off the pulpit and went down right before him there and still couldn't arouse him. Finally I said let's just sing the invitation song and I started the invitation hymn and he woke up about half way through the first verse and was really shocked, so I am going to be watching Paul very closely here this afternoon. We have had marvelous singing today and I appreciate that wonderful prayer in which we were lead. It is a delight to be with the people of God always. I have looked forward to being with you and treasure the experiences we will have together. Tomorrow night at 7:00 p.m. we plan to speak on an old, old subject that we have entitled Saving Faith. If you have to miss any service do not let it be tomorrow night. Just make your plans to come back and be with us tomorrow evening and may be bring someone with you. Maybe a neighbor, friend, coworker, or classmate. Maybe somewhere along the line you can encourage someone to come and be with you.

I want to ask you a question this afternoon. That question is simply this. Do you have somebody that you met along the highway of life that you are unwilling to forgive? Maybe they have so wronged you and so hurt you so deeply that you are just unwilling to forgive them. The Bible is a book about forgiveness. The Bible has a great deal to say about forgiveness. On one occasion, Simon Peter came to Jesus and he posed this question. Lord how many times do I have to forgive my brother who has sinned against me? Do I have to forgive him seven times and Jesus says not seven times but seventy times seven. Then our Lord taught this story. He gave this parable. He says the kingdom of heaven is liken to a certain king who wanted to settle accounts with his servants. They brought one man that owed him 10,000 talents but he was not able to pay and the master commanded that he be sold, that his wife, children, and all that he had taken away from him. The servant fell down before the master and said master have patience with me and I will pay you all. It is like a man that owed 10 million dollars and there is probably no way he is going to be able to repay that debt but he begged for mercy. He begged for opportunity and he begged for some time. The master of this servant was moved with compassion and he released him. He forgave him of the debt but that same servant went out and found one of his fellow servants who owed him 100 dinero, owed him a 100. Dollars or so. He laid his hands on him and took him by the throat saying pay me what you owe me. He begged for leniency. He fell down on his knees and said have patience with me and I will pay you all but he would not, and he threw him into prison until he should pay his debt. When his fellow servant saw what had been done, they were very grieved and they came and told their master all that had been done. The master said, you wicked servant, I forgave you of the debt because you begged me. Should you not have had compassion on your fellow servant just as I had pity on you? His master was angry and delivered him to the torturers until he should pay all that was due him. Now notice this scary verse, So my heavenly father also will do to you if each of you from his heart does not forgive his brother his trespass. I was preaching in Summerville, AL. I had started preaching there when I was a freshman at Freed-Hardeman University. After some time a dear lady came up to me and she said do I have to forgive my sister in the flesh? Do I have to forgive her until she ask for forgiveness? I thought perhaps some wrong had been done to her a week or so ago but to my dismay, the event occurred 25 years ago. This family could not get together on Thanksgiving with all family members present because there had been a break in relationship in the family. They could not come together at Christmas time to exchange gifts. If one found out the other was going to be there, they simply would not show up. What a tragedy this is. That is what unforgiveness does to us. When I was invited by a friend of mine to go up and have a prayer with his father who said my father is dying would you please come up and have a prayer at University Hospital because I do not believe my father is going to survive. I went up and sure enough his father looked like he was at the point of death. He had all kinds of tubes going in him and going out of him and looked like he would not last very long. I said to the sister of this man who was there, lets get the two brothers and you together and lets come and have a prayer together. She said Brother Jerry that will not be possible. You see, my brothers will not speak to one another. It seemed that they lived on adjoining farms and one of them had put a fence over too far on what his brother says was his property, it was about 3 or 4 feet. They came to the same congregation. They sat in the same church building. They sang about their love and devotion to God but they would not speak to one another. They would not meet in the same room and hold hands to pray over their father who was about to be called out into eternity.

Unforgiveness is a horrible thing in our lives. It will destroy relationships. It will destroy families. It will above all destroy our relationship with God. I want to begin this afternoon by talking a little bit concerning some myths about forgiveness. First of all I want to suggest to you that forgiveness is not forgetting. Now our goal should be to forget, God has that ability. He says your sins and your iniquities will I remember against you no more forever. That ought to be our goal but it does not mean that you have not forgiven someone if you still remember the events that occurred. Yet, there are those that say well you have not really genuinely and truly forgiven because if you had really forgiven you would have forgotten all of these things. Forgiveness does not entail the absence of feeling of pain. Whenever you stop feeling you die emotionally. So there will perhaps always be the pain that is there, especially if that wrong has been so severe. Forgiveness is not the total absence of pain. We still may hurt when we remember an event and forgiveness does not involve our doing away with all pain. Forgiveness does not mean you cease longing for justice. We still can long for justice. Vengeance is not a bad thing otherwise, God would be in error. God is a God of vengeance. In Romans chapter 12, the apostle Paul said do not repay one evil for evil. Have regard for good things in the sight of all men. If it is possible as much as it depends on you live peaceably with all men. That ought to be our goal, to live peaceably with all men as much as it is possible. Beloved do not avenge yourself but rather give place to wrath for it is written vengeance is mine, I will repay saith the Lord. So God says I will take care of it if someone has wronged you,

God gives this a promise to his children that you do not have to avenge yourself because God said I will take care of that matter. God has more power. God has more ability than we could ever imagine, certainly more than we have. God has made us a promise if I didn't believe that promise, I wouldn't believe any promise in the Bible. God is not a God who lies. God is not one who endeavors to deceive us. God says I will repay and if somebody has wronged you and treated you unfairly and not done correctly toward you, God says you do not have to retaliate. Vengeance is mine. I will repay saith the Lord. Then Paul said, "If your enemy hungers, feed him. If he thirsts, give him something to drink ,for in so doing thou shall heap coals of fire upon his head." One lady of course had a wrong attitude toward another. The preacher asked her, have you tried heaping coals of fire upon his head by doing good to him? She said I haven't tired coals of fire but I have poured some hot water on him. There are those of us that may be in that category. God says I will take care of the matter. I am saying to you that vengeance does not mean that you no longer seek justice but it does mean that we leave that up to God. One reason that people refuse to forgive is that they believe that to do so would be to minimize the offense and that would not be fair but God says it is fair because I will take care of the matter. Fourthly, forgiveness does not mean that you will make it easier for the offender to hurt you again. I know a lady who in her family has been the walking doormat of her family. Yet, she still makes herself gullible time after time again. We are not to be doormats. It does not mean that we cannot speak up and say that is not fair, you are not treating me properly. We are not to be a doormat. Forgiveness is not to be a one time climatic event. Forgiveness may take a long, long while. It may take sometimes almost a lifetime to be genuinely forgiving of another. We must constantly work on it. It is not just simply something that we do on the spur of the moment. Another truth about forgiveness, Paul says that our forgiveness is to be as God in Christ also forgave us. In Ephesians 4:32, be ye kind, tenderhearted, forgiving one another even as God in Christ also has forgiven you. There are two points that he makes here. We are to forgive because God forgave us. We were condemned, doomed. We were headed toward eternal separation from God because of the wayward life that we live because of our indifferent attitude toward God and the work of God. Yet, the Bible says that God forgave us. We are to forgive the same way that he forgave us. How did God forgive us? He absorbed in himself the destructive pain and the consequence of our sin. Forgiveness is therefore the decision to live with the painful consequences of another person's sin. You are going to have to do it anyway, so you might as well do it without bitterness, rancor, and hatred in our heart toward other human beings. God forgave us in Christ by canceling the debt. We are no longer liable for our sins in the way that we must pay for them. Forgiveness of others means that God has forgiven and he will revoke that wrong that has been done us. Therefore, he says, God says I will take care of this matter. True forgiveness pursues restoration. We try to the best of our ability to restore. True forgiveness longs to love again, however, relationships are built upon trust and trust is not built in a day. In Ephesians 4 he says, restoration and reconciliation are not always possible. Romans 12 Paul says, "In as much as is possible within you." Sometimes it is impossible. Reconciliation is the idea. Forgiveness is the action of one person but reconciliation takes two parties. Our goal should be reconciliation, but it may be that there can only be forgiveness that will be accomplished.

Thirdly, forgiveness endeavors to bury the hatchet. Old Joe was dying and for years he and Bill had been good friends but later in their life they had a falling out. They had wronged one another. They had tried to get it straight between but they could not do so. Now old Joe was dying. He called Bill by his bedside. He told him he was afraid to go out in to eternity with such a bad feeling between them. He was very reluctant to face his maker feeling the way that he did towards Bill. Joe apologized for the things he had said and for the things he had done. He assured Bill that he forgave him of the offenses, everything seemed to be just beautiful but as Bill turned to walk out of the room Joe called to him and said but remember if I get better this doesn't count. Sometimes that is the way we may be. We may smile at this story but forgiveness is often superficial and it is not genuine and not from the heart. Notice what he said, so my heavenly father also will do to you if each of you from his heart, not hypocritical but if you from your heart do not forgive the brother that trespasses. In the book of Ezekiel chapter 36, I will give you a new heart. I will put a new spirit within you and I will take the heart of stone out of your flesh and give you a heart of flesh. I will put my spirit within you and cause you to walk in my statues and you shall keep my commandments and do them. This is what real and genuine forgiveness involves. Our Lord says there was a certain creditor who had two debtors. One owed 500 dinero the other owed 50. When they had done nothing to repay, he freely forgave them both and Jesus said tell me therefore which of them loved the more and of course the answer was the one that had forgiven more. I believe brethren that there is a danger in some of our lives. Those of us who have grown up within the family of God. Sometimes we are not as energized as others are. Sometimes we are not as convicted as others are who accept the gospel may be with no family member or no ties to the church of our Lord. It seems that they really greatly appreciate their redemption and salvation. Where as those of us that may have been brought to services all of our life, in a Bible class, know of the love and grace of God. Sometimes we may feel that we really have not been as mean and ugly as others therefore we do not really need forgiveness. After all, we are pretty good servants of God, even without God's forgiveness. Brethren, nothing could be further from the truth than that. The spirit of lackadaisical-ness. The spirit of luke warmness is a spirit that God does not respect and God does indeed retaliate. Every man ought to have a cemetery in which he buries the faults of his friends and that cemetery ought to be pretty large. All our sins on Him were laid. Christ the Lord our debt has paid. We like him should try to live always ready to forgive. That is the great story of the Bible. The story of forgiveness. The story of God's marvelous ability to forgive us and we need to emulate that to the very best of our ability. What will happen to us if we long to have fellowship with God yet we continue to hold a grudge against a family member, neighbor, or against a friend. Listen to what Jesus said in Mark 6, but if you do not forgive men their trespasses neither will your Father forgive you your trespasses. If you are unwilling to forgive others he says your Heavenly Father will not forgive you. Can you think of someone you need to forgive in your life. In Psalm 139, David said, "Search me Lord, know my thoughts, try me, know my anxieties and see if there is any wickedness in me and lead me in the way everlasting." That ought to be our prayer. Look into my heart and see if there are wrong feelings toward others that I am harboring. Forgiveness means that we release the debt the other party owes and it will cost us. Sometimes we have to deny our rights. Sometimes we can do this out of our attitudes yet not as genuinely as we should. Jesus came our debts to pay, to save our souls in grace one day. So in love we all should live, ready always to forgive. Are you good at forgiving? Have you forgiven others? Think about how much the Lord has forgiven us. Even the generosity of one's forgiveness is not practiced by those that in many ways, are faithful members of the Lord's church. What is the test of our spirituality. Someone says well if I attend all services that is important. Someone says if I give 10, 15, or 20% of our income to God, and certainly that would be remarkable, but I believe the real test of our spirituality is our ability and willingness to forgive others. It is hard for us to forgive a person who has wronged us and who has offended us and yet look at Jesus. Our Lord never wronged anyone and yet look at his attitude. An attitude of being willing to forgive. The more we become like Jesus the easier it will be for us to forgive others. When we think of how much he forgave us, it ought to be easier for us to forgive another. I found a little remedy to ease the life we live. It makes each day a happier one. It is the word forgive. When it seems you cannot forgive, remember how much God has forgiven you. Well, how does God forgive us? David said in Psalm 103, that God has taken our sins and cast them as far as the east is from the west. We measure north and south. We have a north pole and a south pole but we have no east and west pole. I am sure that means that God forgives us in an unlimited way. In Micah chapter 7:19, he says he will take our sins and cast them into the depths of the ocean. How deep is the ocean. Someone has said the ocean is probably 7 miles deep at some points, may be even deeper. We know that God takes our sins and casts them into the depths of the ocean. He takes our sins and puts them away from his abilities to recall. He blots them out of his book of remembrance. When God forgives us, God forgives us of 3 things. He forgives us of the penalty of wrong. The penalty of wrong is to be separated from him eternally. The scripture says that God forgives us for the penalty for wrong. Romans 6:23, "The wages of sin is death but the gift of God is eternal life through Jesus Christ our Lord." He forgives us not only of the penalty, he forgives us of the guilt of wrong as though we had not committed a sin to begin with.

I came to the desk with quivering lips the hole year was done. Dear teacher has thou a new leaf for me for I have spoiled this one. She took that old leaf stained and blotted and gave me a new one all unspotted and into my sad eyes smiled, "Do better my child." I came to the Lord with a quivering soul. The old year was done, dear Father has thy have a new leaf for me I have spoiled this one. He took the old leaf stained and blotted and gave me a new one all unspotted and in to my sad heart smiled, "Do better my child."

I am so grateful that God has a big ole eraser and that when we have wronged him, He erases those sins from our life as we comply with his will of forgiveness. That should be the goal we have toward others. God not only does that but God restores us to full fellowship as though we had not committed a sin to begin with. One old fellow was restored every Sunday after being drunk on Saturday night. Someone came to him and said to him, we are going to have to withdraw our fellowship from you because of the actions you have taken. The old brother did not understand but he said I will carry on the best way I possibly can here, I hope you brethren will come and visit occasionally. Sometimes that is the way we may be, we may have that kind of spirit but we ought to be restoring one to a full fellowship as though they had never committed any sin against us. One young lady came down the isle one Wednesday night, she was crying. She was expecting a little baby and she was not married. Her mother came down the isle and she too was crying. The father also came along. They had a prayer of forgiveness and the congregation gathered around and they all forgave. There was hugging, kissing, love, and fellowship. Some weeks later one of the ladies wanted to give her a shower. The ladies said we cannot do that because to do so would condone her action. I am reminded of the attitude of the older brother when the prodigal came back home seeking to be a servant but the father said kill the fatted calf and bring forth the ring, the robe and sandals because my boy was lost and he is found again. He was dead and he is alive. He was restored to full fellowship. There was a party and after the older brother would not come but called a servant out and had his father come out. He was angry, not because his brother had come back but he was angry because he said you never killed a fatted calf for me. You never gave me a party. That represents the attitude of God and the attitude of genuinely forgiving and restoring us to full fellowship as though we had never done wrong.

My dear grandmother lived until she was 92 years of age. Probably the reason that many of us are preaching in our family. My brother, my sons, and others, is due to the influence of this very Godly woman. When she was 85 on a Sunday afternoon she was lying on the couch getting ready to sleep just a little bit before she went to services that Sunday night. She heard a knock on the door. She went to the door and there was a big fellow standing outside that door. He said mam could I use your phone. She said I do not let strange people into my house and she refused. He said well could I have a drink of water please and you and I both know the scripture she thought about as she made her way shuffling along on the floor to the refrigerator and got him a glass of ice water. He moved away from the door and she set it outside and when she did so, he took hold of the door. He came inside and raped my 85 year old grandmother. She would never get over it. Her sons wanted to kill him. He was found. I will tell you I had a hard time thinking about it but I remember the words of my grandmother. Later in life she said I pray for him every day. He may have ruined my life but I pray that he may hear the gospel of Jesus and become a simple child of God and go to heaven. That is forgiveness.

If you are here today and desire to be forgiven the Bible teaches that through faith that leads you to repent of your wrongs to confess the sweet name of Jesus to be immersed in the watery tomb of baptism God will wipe away all of your sins and make you stand white with him. If you are here today and have a wrong attitude and relationship toward another make it right between you and that other individual as much as you can as we indicated sometimes that is not possible but as much as you can to be sure that you are not the party that is putting on the coals of the fire. Be a forgiving person because God wants you to forgive. Some of these days when we stand before the great God of the universe, He will say you forgave others, I forgive you. Be buried with your Lord in baptism for the forgiveness of your sins. Arise to walk a new life if you walk contrary to his will and to his way and not live as a Christian should live we urge you to come back home. If you would come now as together we stand and sing.

HEAVEN

Dad preached this sermon a few months before he died in one of his last meetings. It is a fitting way to close out his sermons with a lesson on what he lived his life for and spend his life encouraging others toward.

J & D

Thanks to all of you for encouraging and inviting others to come to be a part of this service. Some of you have not missed a single service and we are always grateful for the faithfulness and dedication of those who are so minded. There are those perhaps tonight who are not members of the family of God who are in this assembly. It is our hope and prayer this evening will be that day that you make the most important decision of all your life. The decision to become a simple New Testament Christian. There may be those who are not faithful to God, those who have not been regular in your attendance, or those who come whenever the mood strikes you but do not come with any degree of regularity. Those who may go off on trips and fail to assemble with the saints of God or those who relegate the kingdom of God secondary in their life and travel on Sunday because of a vacation time they have had and leave God the leftovers of the day by coming to the second service to meet around the Lords' table with those who were not able to attend that morning.

The kingdom of God must be first in our life. Matthew 6:33 says, Seek ye first, not second but first. It is more important than school, work and more important than any other relationship that you sustain is that relationship you have with God and with His kingdom or with His church. We are living in a time when the church is not considered very important but it is our hope and prayer as you grow older in the faith and more mature the study of God's will that you will be able to appreciate the kingdom of God as you really should.

Man is a composite being. He is made up of a body, soul, and in Thessalonians Paul says and a spirit. In that particular verse I think that Paul is talking about the body as we all know and the spirit to the eternal part of God and the soul to life, like Adam when God breathed into the nostrils of Adam becoming a living soul. Sometimes the word soul means the same thing as the spirit but in this particular verse, I think that Paul has referenced to the life and to the eternal part of man and to the body itself. So man is a triune being. Man is made up of a part that will live forever and ever and will not die. When you die, there is a part of you that does not die. The body dies and death is when we stop breathing and when the spirit departs from the body. James 2:26 informs us that the body without the spirit it is dead and that is what death really is. When death occurs the spirit has separated itself from the body. It is appointed unto man once to die not seventeen times to die or twelve times to die but it is appointed unto man once to die and after this the judgement. The body we bury in mother earth and the body that is buried will be resurrected. John 5:28-29, the hour is coming in which all that are in the grave will hear his voice and shall come forth; they that have done good unto the resurrection of life; and they that have done evil , unto the resurrection of damnation. The hour is coming when all that are in the grave, the spirit is not in the grave, that is talking about the body. Paul said in 1 Corinthians 15, that which was sown in dishonor will be raised in glory, that which as sown a natural body will be raised a spiritual body, that which was sown in weakness will be raised in power and might. So there will be a bodily resurrection but the spirit goes to God who gave it. The spirit goes to our Father in heaven. There are two compartments according to Luke chapter 16, where man goes immediately upon the point of death one is a place described in Luke 16 as a place of torment, the other is a place is upon Abraham's bosom.

Now some would argue well if that is the case, what is the purpose of the judgement day. Well, you know today whether you are lost or saved. If you have never become a New Testament Christian you will have to wait until the day of judgement to find out if you are lost. If you are unfaithful in service to God, you will not have to wait until the judgement day to find out you are going to be lost. You know you are lost right now. If you are walking with God, the Bible indicates if we are walking with God and we are living the way that God wants us to live then of course, we will be able to know we are saved. 1 John 5, these things I write unto you that you may know you have eternal life, so we can know of our redemption. We can know not in an arrogant, boastful sense. Let him that thinketh he stand take heed lest he fall. We can know we are saved, justified and redeemed by the blood of the Lord. Then those in the judgement day who are righteous will be on the right hand of God and those who are unrighteous will be on the left hand of God. Matthew chapter 25 says, He will separate them. As the shepherd divides the sheep from the goats, the goats on the left hand and the sheep on the right hand. Those on the left hand he will say depart from me ye that work iniquity. I do not know you. Those on the left hand will go into a place that the Bible describes as a place of fire. I do not want to burn to death. I had a little friend. Her name was Betty. She was probably about 5 years of age. Little Betty died, she was scalded to death in a tub of water. I saw her and it is horrible to think about somebody scalding to death. Someone being burned because the water was so hot. I came upon an accident several years ago, I guess it has been 18 years or so ago. There was a couple trapped inside of a car and the car caught on fire and we tried our best to get that couple out. I reached a hold of the door burning my hand

278 - THE LIVING WORD

because it was so hot. This couple were in the fire, begging, pleading for someone to get them out of the fire. Don't you know that in hell there will be weeping, moaning, groaning, and people begging for grace and mercy and that God would redeem them but it will be too late. The Bible describes hell in Matthew 13:41-42 as a furnace of fire. Matthew chapter 25:41 it is referred to as everlasting fire. Revelation 20:15 is a lake of fire. Mark 9:44 it is unquenchable fire. If we are lost, we are going to burn. It will be a place of darkness. Several years ago, I was in North Alabama and someone asked if I wanted on a Sunday afternoon to go back in to a coal mine. They got me some old cloths and I put on those old cloths and I went back in to the coal mine. After we got back there, they cut off those car beam lights and you talk about darkness. I tell you, I would not want to be forever in outer darkness. There will be no light there. No light at all and the sounds of hell. The sounds of weeping. Not the weeping of little children, there will not be any little children in hell. It will be the weeping of grown individuals. Those who are old enough to know what is right and what is wrong. I do not want to go to hell and listen to that sound. The pain will be so intense that there will be gnashing of teeth. People literally grinding their teeth together because of the pain so bad. I don't want to be lost. I don't even want a dog to go to hell. The Bible indicates that we make a choice in going to hell. We decide that we are going to not obey the will of God. There are some things in hell worse than fire. Dante says in the form inferno across the gates of hell should be written these words: Those who enter here will never leave. There is the haunting memory. Think about living throughout eternity and knowing you had opportunity to make changes in your life but you chose not to do so. Then of course, there will be the separation. Mothers separated from their little babies. Husbands and wives. One man said we have never been apart a day in our lives since we have been married, yet they will be apart forever because the woman was a faithful child of God and the husband did not have time to be a Christian that he should be. I don't want to go to hell.

Well tonight, I want to place our primary emphasis upon the other direction that we have been singing about. Jesus was in an upper room and he went around and washed the disciples feet. They protested, especially Peter but so said they all one verse says. He even washed Judas Iscariot's feet. Sometime after that He said, tonight I am going to be betrayed and one of you is going to betray me. They began to ask, Lord is it I?, is it I? Jesus said the one that dips with me in the dish, probably there were several dishes there on the table and may be 4 or 5 dipping out of the same dish he was dipping out of, narrowing the circle even more. In Matthew 26:25, Judas Iscariot said Master is it I? And Jesus said, Thou has said it is you and he of course went out quickly making arrangements for 30 pieces of silver to betray our Lord. Sometime after he had left, Jesus said let not your heart be troubled, ye believe in God, believe also in me. In my Father's house there are many mansions. If it were not so I would have told you. I go to prepare a place for you and if I go I will come again and receive you unto myself, where I am there you may be also. If I had the ability tonight to describe how marvelous heaven would be, there would not be a single person that would want to leave here unless you are sure that you were walking toward heaven. The word heaven is used in 3 senses in the Bible. The word occurs more than 500 times in God's word. There is a heavens where the fouls of the heavens fly, Genesis chapter 1. There is a heavens that we call outer space, Psalms 19:1-2, the heavens declare the glory of God and the firmament sheweth his handiwork. There is a third heaven and that is the one we are primarily interested in tonight. You know the Bible doesn't give us a great amount of description of heaven. We read carefully the book of Genesis and the life of Adam and Eve. We do not know what they might have known about heaven. There is no mention there in those early chapters of Genesis about heaven. We read about Noah who built the ark. We are not aware of what Noah might have known about heaven itself. We come to the life of Abraham and Abraham had some degree of understanding about heaven. The Bible said he looked for a city whose builder and maker is God. So we know he had some concept of heaven. When we close the book of Genesis, those 50 chapters, we do not know a great deal about heaven. In the book of Job, Job said, I know that I shall see God. King James says in my flesh but I think the original has a little bit different bearing on that Job believed some kind of future life and that he would see God after he had departed the walks of this life. The Bible informs us throughout the Old Testament, 39 books, not very much information about this place called heaven. We come to the New Testament and we eagerly read the New Testament to learn what the Bible says about heaven. Jesus of course as we already indicated on one occasion gathered before all nations. We want to listen intently what Jesus is going to say about heaven but he does not tell us a great amount about heaven. We come to 2 Corinthians where Paul said, I knew a man above 14 years ago whether in the body or out of the body I cannot tell but God knows. He was called up into the third heaven. That is the heaven we are interested in. Heaven number one is where the birds fly, heaven number 2 where the sun, moon, stars are and the third heaven the abode of God. Our Father who art in heaven Jesus taught us to pray. We are really eager now to learn about heaven and yet Paul said he saw things that were not permitted for him to tell. We are so disappointed. Heaven. We come all the way down the book of Revelation in chapter 21 there is an unveiling. I really believe he is talking about the church there, that tabernacle that came down out of heaven. Since the church is the vestibule of heaven and heaven will be a magnification of the church. The love, concern and fellowship that we have. The singing, praising of God that we have among the earth will simply be intensified in heaven then we can get some understanding about heaven itself. First of all, the Bible says there are some things that are not going to be in heaven. We like some things that are not going to be present. We don't want to be outdoors when there are a lot of mosquitoes do we or maybe gnats or ants. There are some things that we don't want around us. I begin tonight by mentioning some things that are not going to be in heaven. I would say to you there will not be any pain in heaven. That does not mean a great deal to many who are here tonight, especially those who may be younger who have not experienced a great deal of pain. There are people that do not have a day go by in their life without a high degree of pain. There will be no pain in heaven. Think about living where there will be absolutely no pain at all there. I want to go to a place where there is no pain, no eyeglasses, hearing aids, canes, and no kind of contraptions to help us get around better. There will be none of that in heaven. It will be a place where there is no pain. It will be a place where there is no disease. It will be a place where there is no disease. Present as the will be the redeemer, the great healer, the Balm of Gilead. There will be no cancer in heaven. There will be no heart problems in heaven.

There will be no muscular dystrophy there. There will be no debilitating problems of any kind. This may not mean much to some because you may never have had any kind of sickness to this time in your life but in heaven there will be no kind of pain and no kind of disease. I want to go to heaven because of what is not going to be there. I want to go to heaven because there will be no crime there. I live in a city that crime is common. I have been talking on the phone on more than one occasion and I would hear gunfire ring out and I would know I was talking to someone in a community where crime was taking place. I remember on one occasion a man called me and asked me if I would bring some food over to him because he did not have any food himself and his family. I said I do not believe I need to go in that neighborhood at this time but I will meet you at a certain place. I met him at this place. I felt sorry for him and I said I will take a chance and take you on in to that area where you live. I did, I took him home, got him out of the car and got his food and squared him away. I hadn't been gone 15 minutes and later that night I turned on the television 4 people had been killed in that very area where I was. There will be no crime in heaven. I live in a city where there are 22,000 crimes committed every year. More than 90 murders have been committed, 240 rapes, 12,000 deaths. It is not uncommon to lose an automobile there. We live in a world of crime and crime is caused by an attitude that will not be in heaven. I want to go to heaven because there will be no pain, because there will be no disease, and because there will be no crime. Heaven will be a place where there will be no babies murdered in their mother's womb. No young people destroyed by illicit drugs. No caudaling of criminals, no glorifying of crime in movies, television. No applause of indecent and vulgar performers. No government which tries to convert gambling from a prize to a virtue. No athlete paid millions while homeless people sleep on the streets. No using the name of God in vain. You will never hear that in heaven. The name of God and the name of Jesus will never be taken in vain there. There will be no curse words. There will be no utility bills, broken down automobiles, no headaches, or long lines of delay. No Fs on report cards. No children staying out too late. No hungry or empty food shelves. No wreckers pulling down old broken down automobiles. No crabgrass or Johnson grass. No eviction notices. No caskets. No disappointments. No mournfully sad songs. No hearses leading long funeral processions. In other words, there will be nothing in heaven that will bring unhappiness to anybody. I want to go to heaven and I want all the folks I know to go to heaven. I want everyone in this auditorium on this Wednesday night to go to heaven, without a single exception. We all need to go to heaven. I want to go to heaven because of the wonderful things that are going to be there in heaven. A little blind girl, because of a successful surgeon who came in to the area, the mother of this little blind girl went over and begged. She did not have the money to pay this high power physician but because of his kindness he operated on the little girl. He removed the bandages after 3 days and told her to look. For the first time she looked in the beautiful face of her mother and she went to the window and looked out and saw the green grass. She saw the roses blooming and saw the clouds and the sky. She said oh mother why didn't you tell me it was so beautiful. I am sure that is the way we are going to feel about heaven. Why didn't somebody tell us how beautiful heaven is. In heaven there will be only one street and it will be paved with pure gold. There will be 12 humongous gates, 3 on each side of heaven and these gates will be made out of

gigantic pearls. These gates will never close. The gates of the city
will be 12,000 forlons. I have read one man who said he had
already calculated and heaven had already been filled up so
there was no room for anyone else but this is more than 1500
miles that is not only wide and long 1500 miles, it is 1500 miles
high. There will be a place for everybody who wants to go there.
The walls around heaven are more than 200 feet high. They are
made of jasper. The foundation of these walls are made out of 12
precious and beautiful stones. The light of this city called heaven
is provided by the glory of God. In heaven will be the pure river
of the water of life. There will be no pollution but clear as
crystal proceeding out of the throne of God. In the middle of
the street in heaven on either side will be the tree of life bearing
12 different kinds of fruits. I want to go to heaven because of
what will be there. Love will be in heaven. It will be a place
where all are gentle and where there will be no pride at all.
There will be no arrogance and no selfishness. It will be a place
of purity. It will be a marvelous place with having perfect bodies
and perfect minds. I want to go to heaven because of who is
going to be there. I read about one man and he said when I was
a little boy and I heard preachers talk about heaven, I thought
about the street of gold and I thought about the mansions that
were going to be there but he said I didn't know anybody there.
He said when I was older my little sister who was about 7 or 8
years of age died and I knew that she would go to heaven. He
said I wanted to go to heaven and I thought about the street of
gold. I thought about the mansions that would be there and all
the great jewels that would be there but he said I knew one
person that would be there. I knew my little sister would be
there. He said now I am an old man and he said as an old man I
do not think about the street of gold. I do not think about all

the various kinds of fruit and the tree of Life but he said I think about all of my friends who are going to be there. It will be a place where all of the redeemed of all ages will go. Where there will be those of every kindred and tongue and people. Several years ago, brother S. Tidley, the great song writer, wrote quite a number of songs, perhaps even as we sing here. He was being honored for his 100th birthday in Dallas, TX. They said to this man of all of the songs that you have written, which one is your favorite? Without hesitation he said the song Worthy is the Lamb that was slain to receive power, riches, wisdom, strength, honor, glory, and blessings. He said I love that song most of all of the ones that I have written because that song comes out of the book of Revelation chapter 5.

My question tonight is are you on your way to heaven. I wonder tonight if some of us, may it never happen, leave here and we did not make it to our destination of home could it be said without any doubt at all that indeed we were on our way to heaven? That we would be in heaven forever more. I don't want to be lost in hell. I don't want to experience the horrors and tragedies, burning forever and forever, living in outer darkness. With all the sorry, mean people that will be there. I want to go to heaven where there will be wonderful sweet bliss and happiness forever more.

If you are not prepared to go to heaven, you must have your name written in God's book before you can be there. The Bible said there were those that don't go to heaven, even that have their names in that book because in that judgement day their name will be blotted out of the book of life. God is not going to save you if you do not want to be saved. God is not going to perform some kind of strange, small voice talking in your life and heart saying you need to get right with God. God wants you to be saved. He evidenced that by the giving of His precious Son upon the cross at Calvery. He gave His most precious possession in order that you could spend eternity with Him. What a great God we serve. How we should live for him, love him, and service him every day of our lives. Hebrews chapter 12:23 says to the General assembly and church of the first born whose names are written in heaven. You have to be a member of the church of the first born before your name can be written in heaven. Are you a member of the church that Jesus shed his blood to establish some 2000 years ago? If not, if you trust in Jesus with all of your heart, repent of your sins, confess the sweet name of our Savior and tonight if you will be buried with our Lord in baptism, for the forgiveness of sins, your name will be written down in the book of life. Since 1969 it has been my privilege to go to Central America. I usually go twice a year, in January and March and I preach to people down there. We are on five television stations there so a lot of folks know Jerry Jenkins down there because they watch those television sets. I go down there and preach the gospel and usually there are 15-25 to 30 people who are baptized. Some of these people have never heard the simple message of salvation a single time in their life. When they hear they are obedient to the will of God and they want to become a simple New Testament Christian. I preached to a man one time 15 years and I thought he would never obey the gospel. I thought he might die and all of those sermons and talks we had along with the begging and pleading to make his life right with God, I am happy I had the privilege baptizing him. On the way he lost 3 boys. His boys grew up and were young at receptive age that Daddy did not go to services. They wanted to be like their Daddy. Now not a single one of them, well may be one of them is active in the Lord's church but the others are far removed. Don't wait too late. Your influencing somebody tonight even to go to heaven or hell with you. May it be that it is to go to this land we have described called Heaven. Will you come tonight if you are subject to heaven's call while we stand and sing.

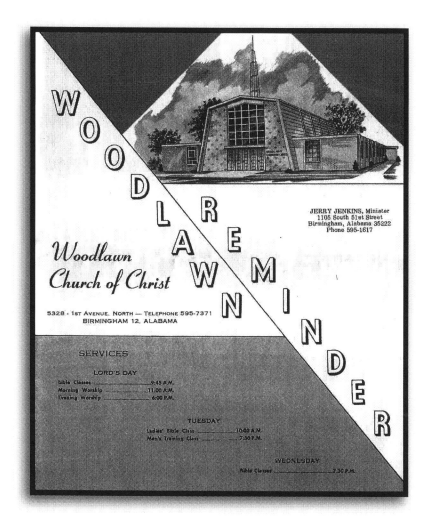

VOLUME I Thursday, OCTOBER 13, 1966 No. 4

FROM THE MINISTER'S PEN

The highest number since February (200), was reached last Sunday in Bible class.

As all of you know we are trying to have "300" present. WILL YOU HELP ? Three Hundred is NOT an unrealistic goal. Presently 270 have been enrolled.

Last Sunday we had 14 visiting. With 200 present this means that 84 classmembers were not present.

At this time 84 members of Woodlawn church of Christ are not enrolled in a class.

THE PERFECT CHURCH

"I think that I shall never see
A church that's all it ought to be:
A church whose members never
    stray
Beyond the straight and narrow
    way;
A church that has no empty pews;
Whose preacher never has the
    blues;
A church whose deacons always
    deak,
And none is proud, and all are
    meek;
Where gossips never peddle lies,
Or make complaints or criticize;
Where all are always sweet and
    kind,
And all to others' faults are blind.
Such perfect churches there may
    be,
But none of them are known to me.
But still, we'll work, and pray and
    plan
To make Woodlawn the best
    we can.
                    Selected & Adapted.

Would You Starve Your Child ?

Would you have the heart to put your children to bed on Saturday night, knowing that they hadn't had a bite to eat all day because of your negligence? You wouldn't?

Then think of putting them to bed on SUNDAY night and looking into their innocent faces, knowing that their souls are starving from having missed services because of your neglect. They are innocent victims of the ones who love them most! The effects of our neglect may be written across their lives in later years in terms of sin, unfaithfulness, and unbelief.

Parent, don't allow this to happen to your children! There is nothing on earth as important as the spiritual training and the good habit of church attendance formed in the early years of a child's life. AS THE TWIG IS BENT SO SHALL THE TREE GROW!

THE   GREATER   SIN   ?

A man goes fishing on Sunday when we are studying God's Word. Another man comes for an hour, but he hasn't studied his lesson. He sits bored and nearly asleep while God's Word is taught, then leaves without learning a thing. Who sins? Who is the greater sinner?

A liquor dealer is struck by a drunken driver. One is responsible for a wrecked car, the other a wrecked life. Who sins in this matter and which is the greater sinner?

A man looks with lust. A woman dresses indecently. Who sins? Who is the greater sinner?

Some men brought an adulteress to Jesus. Before they left He had taught them a great lesson. Have you ever read this lesson? If so, who was the sinner?

IDENTIFYING THE LUKEWARM CHRISTIAN   ! !

1. He has time to read the newspaper everyday, but not the Bible.
2. He spends more time with the sports page than he does in prayer.
3. He spends half as much for entertainment as he gives to the church.
4. He sets a bad example by missing church often.
5. He continually finds falut with those who are trying.
6. He knows he should be giving more, but he loves his money too much.

...because thou art lukewarm....I will spue thee out of my mouth.
(Rev.3:16)

What Some Preachers Say About

Baptism

John Calvin—Presbyterian. "The word baptize signifies to immerse. It is certain that immersion was the practice of the primitive church."

Martin Luther—Lutheran. "Baptism is a Greek word and may be translated immerse. I would have those who are to be baptized to be altogether dipped."

John Wesley—Methodist. "Buried with him in baptism—lluding to the ancient manner of baptizing by immersion."

Wall—Episcopalian. "Immersion was in all probability the way in which our blessed Savior, and for certain the way by which the ancient Christians received their baptism."

Brenner—Catholic. "For thirteen hundred years was baptism an immersion of the person under water."

Macknight—Presbyterian. "In baptism the baptized person is buried under the water. Christ submitted to be baptized, that is, to be buried under water."

Whitfield—Methodist. "It is certain that the word of our text, Romans 6:4, alludes to the manner of baptizing by immersion."

NEWS and NOTES

We regret to announce that one of our fine families is moving out of Birmingham. Mr. & Mrs. Allen Lay will be away for 6 months but they do plan to return. Allen will be on a tour of duty with the Army. Susan will be staying with her parents in Tupelo, Mississippi. Our prayers are with this young couple and we look forward to them returning to Birmingham.

The gospel meeting began at Shannon Church of Christ October 16th and will continue through October 23rd. The speaker will be Ronald L. Hill of Huston, Texas. EVERYONE IS INVITED.

Mary Walters was identified with the congregation Sunday. She lives at: 5110 18th Avenue North. We welcome her to our family.

 DEATH

Our deepest sympathy to the Courington family in the passing of Sloan Estes. The funeral was Sunday at Elmwood Chapel. Mr. Estes was the brother-in-law of sister Courington.

Don't forget the storeroom. Please bring this week: Canned Peaches

 IN THE MAIL

Dear Friends of the Woodlawn Church of Christ. I wish to thank you for the lovely flowers that are being enjoyed so very much.

Bernice Reid

THE RECORD

Service	Sunday	Year Ago
Little Folks Class	34	
Bible School	200	165
11 AM Worship	244	192
Evening Worship	145	125
Wednesday	105	92
Contribution	$1010.00	$692.00

Hospital News

Larry Wiley, Mary Wileys son, underwent a tonsillectomy early this week.

++

A.M. "THE WORST SIN ONE CAN COMMIT"

P.M. "TEMPERANCE"

++

CAN YOU RECOMMEND YOUR RELIGION?

Published weekly by the Woodlawn Church of Christ, 5328 First Avenue North, Birmingham, Ala. 35212

APPLICATION FOR SECOND-CLASS MAIL PRIVILEGES PENDING AT BIRMINGHAM, ALABAMA,

Woodlawn Church of Christ
5328 1st Avenue North
Birmingham, Alabama 35212

Name

Also from the Jenkins Institute:

Thoughts From the Mound
The Glory of Preaching
Before I Go: Notes from Older Preachers

All I Ever Wanted to Do Was Preach
I Hope You Have to Pinch Yourself

Five Secrets and a Decision
Centered: Marking Your Map in a Muddled World
Me, You, and the People in the Pews

A Minister's Heart
A Youth Minister's Heart
A Mother's Heart
A Father's Heart

To order, visit thejenkinsinstitute.com/shop

Made in the USA
Columbia, SC
15 August 2022

65401607R00174